This journal is intended for personal documentation purposes only.

It does not constitute legal, medical, financial, or professional advice.
Use of this publication does not create any professional-client relationship. Always seek appropriate professional advice regarding your individual circumstances.

ISBN: 978-1-7645347-8-9

Published by
Healing Storybook Publishers
Australia

www.healingstorybook.com

Insurance Claim Journal

Injury, Compensation & Documentation Log

Healing Storybook Publishers

About This Journal

This journal was developed from first hand experience navigating a complex compensation claim, where one lesson became clear:
people are advised to "document everything,"
yet rarely shown how.

Clear, consistent documentation is not optional in an insurance or compensation claim — it is foundational.
Conversations, medical findings, financial impacts,
and daily limitations often become significant over time.

This journal provides a structured framework to help you record relevant information in a clear, chronological, and consistent manner.
It is a documentation tool only. It does not constitute legal or medical advice.

How To Use This Journal

- Record information as soon as possible after events occur. Record summarised detail of ALL conversations with insurer, no matter how minor they seem.
- Be factual and specific.
Avoid speculation.
- Use consistent scales (e.g., Pain 0–10).
- Retain original copies of certificates, receipts, and reports separately.
- Store this journal securely.

INDEX

CLAIM SNAPSHOT

Claim Overview

CLAIM OVERVIEW

- ☐ Workers Compensation
- ☐ Motor Velricle Accident
- ☐ Public Liability
- ☐ Income Protection
- ☐ Total & Permanent Disability (TPD)
- ☐ Medical Negligence
- ☐ Other: ______________________

Date of Incident: ____________________ Date Claim Lodged: ____________________

Claim Number: ____________________ Policy Number: ____________________

Insurer / Scheme: ____

Case Manager Name: ____

Case Manager *Contact:* Phone: ______________ Email: ____________________

Employer *(if applicable)*: ____

Legal Representative: ________________ Contact: ____________________

CURRENT STATUS

Current Work Capacity: ☐ Pre-injury duties ☐ *Suitable / modified duties* ☐ *No current capacity* ☐ Not applicable

Current Weekly Benefit: ______________________________

Primary Treating Doctor: ______________________________

Next Appointment Date: ______________________________

Next Known Deadline: ______________________________

KEY CLAIM NOTES:

____

____

____

SECTION 2 – INCIDENT SUMMARY

Incident Summary (Facts Only)

Who / What / When / Where / How

Keep it factual. *(Paste a copy of incident report if available)*

CLAIM OVERVIEW

Date of Incident: ______________________________

Date Claim Lodged: ______________________________

Claim Number: ______________________________

Policy Number: ______________________________

Insurer / Scheme: ______________________________

Case Manager Name: ______________________________

Case Manager Contact: ______________________________

______________ Phone: ______________ Email: ______________

Employer *(if applicable)*: ______________________________

CURRENT STATUS

Current Work Capacity: ______________________________

____

____

Current Weekly Benefit: ______________________________

____

Primary Treating Doctor: ______________________________

Next Appointment Date: ______________________________

Next Known Deadline: ______________________________

____

____

Evidence & Document Tracker

(Documents Submitted)

Use this page to record documents you submit in support of your claim.

By keeping a detailed log, you can avoid resending the same documents and prevent forgetting what you've already sent.

Documents Submitted

Document	Date Sent	Sent To	Email	Method	Confirmation Received	Notes
					☐ Yes ☐ No	
					☐ Yes ☐ No	
					☐ Yes ☐ No	
					☐ Yes ☐ No	
					☐ Yes ☐ No	
					☐ Yes ☐ No	

Examples of Documents to Record

- Medical reports
- Treatment plans
- Receipts
- Specialist reports
- Certificates of capacity

Claim Tip

Keeping a clear record of submitted documents:

- Record the reason for the visit
- Document any diagnosis or medical opinions
- Note if the report was sent to insurer

This summary can be extremely useful when reviewing your claim or responding to insurer inquiries such as:

- "When did you first see the psychdogist?"
- "Who diagnosed the injury?"

Claim Timeline Summary

(Chronology of Key Claim Events)

Insurance and compensation claims often extend over months or years. Important events can become difficult to track over time.

This page allows you to record a clear chronological timeline of the key events in your claim.

Keeping an accurate timeline can assist when communicating with insurers, doctors, lawyers, or during dispute resolution.

Claim Timeline Record

Date Event Source / Evidence Notes

<u>Examples of Events to Record</u>

- Injury date
- Claim lodged
- First GP appointment
- First specialist appointment
- Treatment request submitted
- Determination received
- Determination declined
- Redetermination requested
- Independent Medical Examination (IME)
- Case manager change
- Return-to-work assessment
- Legal advice sought
- Tribunal or hearing date

Claim Tip

Maintaining a clear timeline can help identify:

- delays in treatment approvals
- claim decision dates
- changes in medical opinion
- communication patterns with the insurer.

A well-documented timeline can become valuable evidence if a claim is reviewed or disputed.

CLAIM TIMELINE SUMMARY

Chronology of Key Claim Events

Insurance and compensation claims often extend over months or years. Important events can become difficult to track over time.

Use this page to record a simple chronological timeline of key events in your claim as they occur.

Maintaining an accurate timeline can assist when communicating with insurers, doctors, lawyers, or during dispute resolution.

Examples of Events to Record

- Injury date
- Claim lodged
- First GP appointment
- First psychologist appointment
- Treatment request submitted
- Determination received
- Redetermination requested
- Independent medical examination
- Case manager change
- Return-to-work assessment
- Tribunal or legal review

Claim Tip

Recording events as they occur helps create a clear chronological record of the claim, which can become extremely helpful if decisions are reviewed or disputed.
After a year or two, you'll have a perfect timeline automatically built.

Example:

Date	Event	Evidence	Notes
12 Mar 2024	Requested physio	Email to case manager	Awaiting determination
20 Mar 2024	Determination received	Insurer letter	Treatment declined
22 Mar 2024	Redetermination requested	Email sent	Within 30 day period

Claim Timeline Summary

Chronology of Key Claim Events

Insurance and compensation claims often extend over months or years. Important events can become difficult to track over time.

Use this page to record a simple chronological timeline'oe of key events in your claim as they occur.

Maintaining an accurate timeline can assist when communicating with insurers, doctors, lawyers, or during dispute resolution.

Claim Timeline

Date	Event	Evidence / Source	Notes

Examples of Events to Record

- Injury date
- Claim lodged
- First GP appointment
- First psychologist appointment
- Treatment request submitted
- Determination received
- Redetermination requested
- Independent medical examination
- Case manager change
- Return-to-work assessment
- Tribunal or legal review

Claim Tip

Recording events as they occur helps create a clear chronological record of the claim, which can become extremely helpful when decisions are reviewed or disputed.

Case Manager Change Log

This happens constantly in claims. People end up dealing with five or six case managers and lose track of who said what.

- Case Manager Record
- Case Manager Company Phone Email Start Date End Date Notes
- If your case manager changes, record the new contact details and the date they took over your claim.

Evidence & Document Tracker

- Documents Submitted
- Document Date Sent Sent To Method Confirmation Received Notes

Examples:
- medical reports
- treatment plans
- receipts
- specialist reports
- certificates of capacity
- People often forget what they already sent.

Appointment & Medical Report Tracker

Insurance claims often rely heavily on medical reports, and people forget which doctor wrote what.

Medical Appointments
- Date Doctor / Specialist Reason Report Sent to Insurer Notes
- This becomes extremely helpful later when someone asks:
- "When did you first see the psychologist?"
- "Who diagnosed the injury?"

Case Manager Change Log

(Claim Contact Record)

Insurance claims often involve multiple case managers over time.

Use this page to record each case manager assigned to your claim, including their contact details and the dates they managed your case.

Keeping a clear record can help track communication and accountability if issues arise during the claim process.

Case Manager Record

Case Manager	Company / Insurer	Phone	Email	Start Date	Start Date	Handover Confirmed
						☐ Yes ☐ No
						☐ Yes ☐ No
						☐ Yes ☐ No
						☐ Yes ☐ No
						☐ Yes ☐ No

Notes / Important Details

- Record any relevant information about case manager transitions:
  - Reason for the change (if known)
  - Any unresolved issues at the time e of the transition
  - New instructions provided by the incoming case manager
  - Differences in communication or decisions

Notes / Important Details

- Record any relevant information about case manager transitions:
- Reason for the change (if known)
- Any unresolved issues at the time of the transition
- New instructions provided by the incoming case manager
- Differences in communication or decisions

Claim Tip

If your case manager changes, request written confirmation of the new contact details and record the date they assumed responsibility for your claim.

Keeping a clear contact timeline can help avoid misunderstandings and ensure accoumability during the claim process.

Appointment & Medical Report Tracker

Summary of Medical Evidence

Insurance and compensation claims often rely heavily on medical reports.

Use this page to record a chronological summary of medical appointments and reports in your claim.

A clear record of doctor visits and medical reports helps establish the *medical evidence* supporting your claim and makes it easier to find important information later in the claim process.

Medical Appointment & Report Record

Date	Doctor / Specialist	Provider Type	Reason for Appointment	Diagnosis or Opinion Given	Report Sent to Insurer	Notes
					☐ Yes ☐ No	
					☐ Yes ☐ No	
					☐ Yes ☐ No	
					☐ Yes ☐ No	
					☐ Yes ☐ No	
					☐ Yes ☐ No	
					☐ Yes ☐ No	
					☐ Yes ☐ No	

Common Provider Types

- GP (General Practitioner)
- Psychologist
- Psychiatrist
- Physiotherapist
- Specialist Surgeon
- Pain Specialist
- Occupational Therapist
- Independent Medical Examiner (IME)

Claim Tip

After each medical appointment:

- Record the reason for the visit
- Document any diagnosis or medical opinions
- Note if the report was sent to the insurer

This summary can be extremely useful when reviewing your claim or responding to insurer inquiries such as:

- "When did you first see the psychologist?"
- "Who diagnosed the injury?"

Appointment & Medical Report Tracker

Summary of Medical Evidence

Insurance and compensation claims often rely heavily on medical reports.

Use this page to record a chronological summary of medical appointments and reports in your claim.

A clear record of doctor visits and medical reports helps establish the *medical evidence* supporting your claim and makes it easier to find important information later in the claim process.

Medical Appointment & Report Record

Date	Doctor / Specialist	Provider Type	Reason for Appointment	Diagnosis or Opinion Given	Report Sent to Insurer	Notes
					☐ Yes ☐ No	
					☐ Yes ☐ No	
					☐ Yes ☐ No	
					☐ Yes ☐ No	
					☐ Yes ☐ No	
					☐ Yes ☐ No	
					☐ Yes ☐ No	
					☐ Yes ☐ No	

Common Provider Types

- GP (General Practitioner)
- Psychologist
- Psychiatrist
- Physiotherapist
- Specialist Surgeon
- Pain Specialist
- Occupational Therapist
- Independent Medical Examiner (IME)

Claim Tip

After each medical appointment:

- Record the reason for the visit
- Document any diagnosis or medical opinions
- Note if the report was sent to the insurer

This summary can be extremely useful when reviewing your claim or responding to insurer inquiries such as:

- "When did you first see the psychologist?"
- "Who diagnosed the injury?"

Expense & Out-of-Pocket Tracker

A lot of injured workers forget to record expenses they can claim.

Use this page to record any out-of-pocket costs and reimbursable expenses related to your injury or claim.

Claim Expenses

Date	Expense	Amount	Receipt Sent	Reimbursed	Notes
			☐ Yes ☐ No	☐ Yes ☐ No	
			☐ Yes ☐ No	☐ Yes ☐ No	
			☐ Yes ☐ No	☐ Yes ☐ No	
			☐ Yes ☐ No	☐ Yes ☐ No	
			☐ Yes ☐ No	☐ Yes ☐ No	
			☐ Yes ☐ No	☐ Yes ☐ No	
			☐ Yes ☐ No	☐ Yes ☐ No	
			☐ Yes ☐ No	☐ Yes ☐ No	

Examples of Expenses to Record

- Medication
- Travel to Appointments
- Parking
- Medical Equipment

Expense & Out-of-Pocket Tracker

A lot of injured workers forget to record expenses they can claim.

Use this page to record any out-of-pocket costs and reimbursable expenses related to your injury or claim.

Claim Expenses

Date	Expense	Amount	Receipt Sent	Reimbursed	Notes
			☐ Yes ☐ No	☐ Yes ☐ No	
			☐ Yes ☐ No	☐ Yes ☐ No	
			☐ Yes ☐ No	☐ Yes ☐ No	
			☐ Yes ☐ No	☐ Yes ☐ No	
			☐ Yes ☐ No	☐ Yes ☐ No	
			☐ Yes ☐ No	☐ Yes ☐ No	
			☐ Yes ☐ No	☐ Yes ☐ No	
			☐ Yes ☐ No	☐ Yes ☐ No	

Examples of Expenses to Record

- Medication
- Travel to Appointments
- Parking
- Medical Equipment

Expense & Out-of-Pocket Tracker

A lot of injured workers forget to record expenses they can claim.

Use this page to record any out-of-pocket costs and reimbursable expenses related to your injury or claim.

Claim Expenses

Date	Expense	Amount	Receipt Sent	Reimbursed	Notes
			☐ Yes ☐ No	☐ Yes ☐ No	
			☐ Yes ☐ No	☐ Yes ☐ No	
			☐ Yes ☐ No	☐ Yes ☐ No	
			☐ Yes ☐ No	☐ Yes ☐ No	
			☐ Yes ☐ No	☐ Yes ☐ No	
			☐ Yes ☐ No	☐ Yes ☐ No	
			☐ Yes ☐ No	☐ Yes ☐ No	
			☐ Yes ☐ No	☐ Yes ☐ No	

Examples of Expenses to Record

Medication	Travel to Appointments
Parking	Medical Equipment

Expense & Out-of-Pocket Tracker

A lot of injured workers forget to record expenses they can claim.

Use this page to record any out-of-pocket costs and reimbursable expenses related to your injury or claim.

Claim Expenses

Date	Expense	Amount	Receipt Sent	Reimbursed	Notes
			☐ Yes ☐ No	☐ Yes ☐ No	
			☐ Yes ☐ No	☐ Yes ☐ No	
			☐ Yes ☐ No	☐ Yes ☐ No	
			☐ Yes ☐ No	☐ Yes ☐ No	
			☐ Yes ☐ No	☐ Yes ☐ No	
			☐ Yes ☐ No	☐ Yes ☐ No	
			☐ Yes ☐ No	☐ Yes ☐ No	
			☐ Yes ☐ No	☐ Yes ☐ No	

Examples of Expenses to Record

- Medication
- Travel to Appointments
- Parking
- Medical Equipment

DETERMINATION & DECISION TRACKER

(Claim Compliance Checklist)

Insurance and workers compensation claims require insurers to provide formal determinations on treatment requests and claim deci-

Recording when requests were made and when determinations were issued can become important evidence if delays or failures occur.

Use this page to track requests and whether a formal determination has been provided.

Record all communication attempts, even when no response is received.

Failure to provide a determination, delays in decision-making, or lack of communication may become relevant during a claim review, legal process, or dispute resolution.

REQUEST SUBMITTED

Request Type	Request Submitted	Determination Received		Date Received
		☐ Yes	☐ Yes No	
Medical Treatment		☐ Yes ☐ No	☐ Yes ☐ No	
Psychological Treatment		☐ Yes ☐ No	☐ Yes ☐ No	
Physiotherapy		☐ Yes ☐ No	☐ Yes ☐ No	
Hospital / Surgery		☐ Yes ☐ No	☐ Yes ☐ No	
Medication		☐ Yes ☐ No	☐ Yes ☐ No	
Diagnostic Tests (MRI /X-Ray etc.)		☐ Yes ☐ No	☐ Yes ☐ No	
Mental Health Program		☐ Yes ☐ No	☐ Yes ☐ No	
Specialist Referral		☐ Yes ☐ No	☐ Yes ☐ No	

Record all communication attempts, even when no response is received.

Failure to provide a determination, delays in decision-making, or lack of communication may become relevant during a claim review, legal process, or dispute resolution.

Determination & Decision Tracker

(Claim Compliance Checklist)

Insurance and workers compensation claims require insurers to provide formal determinations on treatment requests and claim deci-

Recording when requests were made and when determinations were issued can become important evidence if delays or failures occur.

Use this page to track requests and whether a formal determination has been provided.

Record all communication attempts, even when no response is received.

Failure to provide a determination, delays in decision-making, or lack of communication may become relevant during a claim review, legal process, or dispute resolution.

Request Submitted

Request Type	Request Submitted	Determination Received		Date Received
		☐ Yes	☐ Yes No	
Medical Treatment		☐ Yes ☐ No	☐ Yes ☐ No	
Psychological Treatment		☐ Yes ☐ No	☐ Yes ☐ No	
Physiotherapy		☐ Yes ☐ No	☐ Yes ☐ No	
Hospital / Surgery		☐ Yes ☐ No	☐ Yes ☐ No	
Medication		☐ Yes ☐ No	☐ Yes ☐ No	
Diagnostic Tests (MRI /X-Ray etc.)		☐ Yes ☐ No	☐ Yes ☐ No	
Mental Health Program		☐ Yes ☐ No	☐ Yes ☐ No	
Specialist Referral		☐ Yes ☐ No	☐ Yes ☐ No	

Record all communication attempts, even when no response is received.

Failure to provide a determination, delays in decision-making, or lack of communication may become relevant during a claim review, legal process, or dispute resolution.

DETERMINATION & DECISION TRACKER

(Claim Compliance Checklist)

Insurance and workers compensation claims require insurers to provide formal determinations on treatment requests and claim deci-

Recording when requests were made and when determinations were issued can become important evidence if delays or failures occur.

Use this page to track requests and whether a formal determination has been provided.

Record all communication attempts, even when no response is received.

Failure to provide a determination, delays in decision-making, or lack of communication may become relevant during a claim review, legal process, or dispute resolution.

REQUEST SUBMITTED

Request Type	Request Submitted	Determination Received ☐ Yes	☐ Yes No	Date Received
Medical Treatment		☐ Yes ☐ No	☐ Yes ☐ No	
Psychological Treatment		☐ Yes ☐ No	☐ Yes ☐ No	
Physiotherapy		☐ Yes ☐ No	☐ Yes ☐ No	
Hospital / Surgery		☐ Yes ☐ No	☐ Yes ☐ No	
Medication		☐ Yes ☐ No	☐ Yes ☐ No	
Diagnostic Tests (MRI /X-Ray etc.)		☐ Yes ☐ No	☐ Yes ☐ No	
Mental Health Program		☐ Yes ☐ No	☐ Yes ☐ No	
Specialist Referral		☐ Yes ☐ No	☐ Yes ☐ No	

Record all communication attempts, even when no response is received.

Failure to provide a determination, delays in decision-making, or lack of communication may become relevant during a claim review, legal process, or dispute resolution.

Determination & Decision Tracker

(Claim Compliance Checklist)

Insurance and workers compensation claims require insurers to provide formal determinations on treatment requests and claim deci-

Recording when requests were made and when determinations were issued can become important evidence if delays or failures occur.

Use this page to track requests and whether a formal determination has been provided.

Record all communication attempts, even when no response is received.

Failure to provide a determination, delays in decision-making, or lack of communication may become relevant during a claim review, legal process, or dispute resolution.

Request Submitted

Request Type	Request Submitted	Determination Received		Date Received
		☐ Yes	☐ Yes No	
Medical Treatment		☐ Yes ☐ No	☐ Yes ☐ No	
Psychological Treatment		☐ Yes ☐ No	☐ Yes ☐ No	
Physiotherapy		☐ Yes ☐ No	☐ Yes ☐ No	
Hospital / Surgery		☐ Yes ☐ No	☐ Yes ☐ No	
Medication		☐ Yes ☐ No	☐ Yes ☐ No	
Diagnostic Tests (MRI /X-Ray etc.)		☐ Yes ☐ No	☐ Yes ☐ No	
Mental Health Program		☐ Yes ☐ No	☐ Yes ☐ No	
Specialist Referral		☐ Yes ☐ No	☐ Yes ☐ No	

Record all communication attempts, even when no response is received.

Failure to provide a determination, delays in decision-making, or lack of communication may become relevant during a claim review, legal process, or dispute resolution.

Determinations, Delays & Redeterminations

(Recording Decisions and Disputes)

Insurance and workers compensation claims rely on formal determinations. A determination is a written decision from the insurer regarding treatment, benefits, or claim matters.

Determinations should normally be issued within legislated timeframes once a request has been made.

If a decision is delayed, or if you disagree with a decision, it is important to record the issue and follow it up in writing.

If a Determination Is Delayed

If you have requested treatment or approval and have not received a determinatuon within the expected timeframe:

- Follow up with the insurer or *case manager*
- Request an update in writing *(email or letter)*
- Record the date of the *follow-up*
- Keep copies of all correspondence

Keeping a clear timeline may become important if delays *affect* your treatment or claim.

If You Disagree With a Decision

If you disagree with a determination:

- Record the decision you are disputing
- Notify the insurer in writing that you are requesting a *redetermination or review*
- Keep copies of all emails or letters sent
- Record the date the request was submitted

A phone conversation alone may not create a reliable record.

Important Tip

If a case manager advises verbally that something will not be approved, request that the decision be provided as a formal written determination.

Determinations, Delays & Redeterminations (Recording Decisions and Disputes)

Insurance and workers compensation claims rely on formal determinations.
A determination is a written decision from the insurer regarding treatment, benefits, or claim matters.

- Determinations should normally be issued within legislated timeframes once a request has been made.
- If a decision is delayed, or if you disagree with a decision, it is important to record the issue and follow it up in writing.

If a Determination Is Delayed

If you have requested treatment or approval and have not received a determination within the expected timeframe:

- Follow up with the insurer or case manager
- Request an update in writing (email or letter)
- Record the date of the follow-up
- Keep copies of all correspondence
- Keeping a clear timeline may become important if delays affect your treatment or claim.

If You Disagree With a Decision

If you disagree with a determination:

- Record the decision you are disputing
- Notify the insurer in writing that you are requesting a redetermination or review
- Keep copies of all emails or letters sent
- Record the date the request was submitted
- A phone conversation alone may not create a reliable record.

Important Tip

If a case manager advises verbally that something will not be approved, request that the decision be provided as a formal written determination.
This ensures there is a clear record of the decision and the date it was made.

Communication Record

□ Email sent
□ Letter sent
□ Portal submission
□ Supporting documents attached

File location / copy stored: _______________

Personal Note

Disputing a decision does not mean you are being difficult.
It simply ensures that your concerns and evidence are formally recorded.
Clear records can become important if a claim is later reviewed, reconsidered, or examined by legal representatives.

Decision Being Disputed	**Date Determination**	**Date Redetermination**	**Method (Email / Letter /**	**Response Received**	**Notes**

Decision Being Disputed	**Date Determination Received**	**Date Redetermination**	**Method (Email / Letter /**	**Response Received**	**Notes**

Personal Reminder

Clear written records help create a timeline of events during your claim. These records may become helpful if a claim is later reviewed, disputed, or examined by legal or union representatives.

SECTION 3 – COMMUNICATION LOG

Incident Summary (Facts Only)

Who / What / When / Where / How

Keep it factual. *(Paste a copy of incident report if available)*

Date: ______________________

Time: ______________________

Method: ☐ Phone ☐ Email ☐ In Person ☐ Letter

Contact Person: ______________________

Organisation: ______________________

SUMMARY (Facts Only)

ACTIONS PROPOSED BY THEM:

FOLLOW-UP REQUIRED BY ME:

DEADLINE: ______________________

SECTION 3 – COMMUNICATION LOG

Incident Summary (Facts Only)

Who / What / When / Where / How

Keep it factual. *(Paste a copy of incident report if available)*

Date: ______________________

Time: ______________________

Method: ☐ Phone ☐ Email ☐ In Person ☐ Letter

Contact Person: ______________________

Organisation: ______________________

SUMMARY (Facts Only)

ACTIONS PROPOSED BY THEM:

FOLLOW-UP REQUIRED BY ME:

DEADLINE: ______________________

SECTION 3 – COMMUNICATION LOG

Incident Summary (Facts Only)

Who / What / When / Where / How

Keep it factual. *(Paste a copy of incident report if available)*

Date: ______________________

Time: ______________________

Method: ☐ Phone ☐ Email ☐ In Person ☐ Letter

Contact Person: ______________________

Organisation: ______________________

SUMMARY (Facts Only)

ACTIONS PROPOSED BY THEM:

FOLLOW-UP REQUIRED BY ME:

DEADLINE: ______________________

SECTION 3 – COMMUNICATION LOG

Incident Summary (Facts Only)

Who / What / When / Where / How

Keep it factual. *(Paste a copy of incident report if available)*

Date: ______________________

Time: ______________________

Method: ☐ Phone ☐ Email ☐ In Person ☐ Letter

Contact Person: ______________________

Organisation: ______________________

SUMMARY (Facts Only)

ACTIONS PROPOSED BY THEM:

FOLLOW-UP REQUIRED BY ME:

DEADLINE: ______________________

SECTION 3 – COMMUNICATION LOG

Incident Summary (Facts Only)
Who / What / When / Where / How
Keep it factual. *(Paste a copy of incident report if available)*

Date: ______
Time: ______
Method: ☐ Phone ☐ Email ☐ In Person ☐ Letter
Contact Person: ______
Organisation: ______

SUMMARY (Facts Only)

ACTIONS PROPOSED BY THEM:

FOLLOW-UP REQUIRED BY ME:

DEADLINE: ______

SECTION 3 – COMMUNICATION LOG

Incident Summary (Facts Only)
Who / What / When / Where / How
Keep it factual. *(Paste a copy of incident report if available)*

Date: ______
Time: ______
Method: ☐ Phone ☐ Email ☐ In Person ☐ Letter
Contact Person: ______
Organisation: ______

SUMMARY (Facts Only)

ACTIONS PROPOSED BY THEM:

FOLLOW-UP REQUIRED BY ME:

DEADLINE: ______

SECTION 3 – COMMUNICATION LOG

Incident Summary (Facts Only)
Who / What / When / Where / How
Keep it factual. *(Paste a copy of incident report if available)*

Date: ______
Time: ______
Method: ☐ Phone ☐ Email ☐ In Person ☐ Letter
Contact Person: ______
Organisation: ______

SUMMARY (Facts Only)

ACTIONS PROPOSED BY THEM:

FOLLOW-UP REQUIRED BY ME:

DEADLINE: ______

SECTION 3 – COMMUNICATION LOG

Incident Summary (Facts Only)
Who / What / When / Where / How
Keep it factual. *(Paste a copy of incident report if available)*

Date: ______
Time: ______
Method: ☐ Phone ☐ Email ☐ In Person ☐ Letter
Contact Person: ______
Organisation: ______

SUMMARY (Facts Only)

ACTIONS PROPOSED BY THEM:

FOLLOW-UP REQUIRED BY ME:

DEADLINE: ______

SECTION 3 – COMMUNICATION LOG

Incident Summary (Facts Only)

Who / What / When / Where / How

Keep it factual. *(Paste a copy of incident report if available)*

Date: ____________________

Time: ____________________

Method: ☐ Phone ☐ Email ☐ In Person ☐ Letter

Contact Person: ____________________

Organisation: ____________________

SUMMARY (Facts Only)

ACTIONS PROPOSED BY THEM:

FOLLOW-UP REQUIRED BY ME:

DEADLINE: ____________________

SECTION 3 – COMMUNICATION LOG

Incident Summary (Facts Only)

Who / What / When / Where / How

Keep it factual. *(Paste a copy of incident report if available)*

Date: ____________________

Time: ____________________

Method: ☐ Phone ☐ Email ☐ In Person ☐ Letter

Contact Person: ____________________

Organisation: ____________________

SUMMARY (Facts Only)

ACTIONS PROPOSED BY THEM:

FOLLOW-UP REQUIRED BY ME:

DEADLINE: ____________________

SECTION 3 – COMMUNICATION LOG

Incident Summary (Facts Only)

Who / What / When / Where / How

Keep it factual. *(Paste a copy of incident report if available)*

Date: ____________________

Time: ____________________

Method: ☐ Phone ☐ Email ☐ In Person ☐ Letter

Contact Person: ____________________

Organisation: ____________________

SUMMARY (Facts Only)

ACTIONS PROPOSED BY THEM:

FOLLOW-UP REQUIRED BY ME:

DEADLINE: ____________________

SECTION 3 – COMMUNICATION LOG

Incident Summary (Facts Only)

Who / What / When / Where / How

Keep it factual. *(Paste a copy of incident report if available)*

Date: ____________________

Time: ____________________

Method: ☐ Phone ☐ Email ☐ In Person ☐ Letter

Contact Person: ____________________

Organisation: ____________________

SUMMARY (Facts Only)

ACTIONS PROPOSED BY THEM:

FOLLOW-UP REQUIRED BY ME:

DEADLINE: ____________________

SECTION 3 – COMMUNICATION LOG

Incident Summary (Facts Only)
Who / What / When / Where / How
Keep it factual. *(Paste a copy of incident report if available)*

Date: ______
Time: ______
Method: ☐ Phone ☐ Email ☐ In Person ☐ Letter
Contact Person: ______
Organisation: ______

SUMMARY (Facts Only)

ACTIONS PROPOSED BY THEM:

FOLLOW-UP REQUIRED BY ME:

DEADLINE: ______

SECTION 3 – COMMUNICATION LOG

Incident Summary (Facts Only)
Who / What / When / Where / How
Keep it factual. *(Paste a copy of incident report if available)*

Date: ______
Time: ______
Method: ☐ Phone ☐ Email ☐ In Person ☐ Letter
Contact Person: ______
Organisation: ______

SUMMARY (Facts Only)

ACTIONS PROPOSED BY THEM:

FOLLOW-UP REQUIRED BY ME:

DEADLINE: ______

SECTION 3 – COMMUNICATION LOG

Incident Summary (Facts Only)
Who / What / When / Where / How
Keep it factual. *(Paste a copy of incident report if available)*

Date: ______
Time: ______
Method: ☐ Phone ☐ Email ☐ In Person ☐ Letter
Contact Person: ______
Organisation: ______

SUMMARY (Facts Only)

ACTIONS PROPOSED BY THEM:

FOLLOW-UP REQUIRED BY ME:

DEADLINE: ______

SECTION 3 – COMMUNICATION LOG

Incident Summary (Facts Only)
Who / What / When / Where / How
Keep it factual. *(Paste a copy of incident report if available)*

Date: ______
Time: ______
Method: ☐ Phone ☐ Email ☐ In Person ☐ Letter
Contact Person: ______
Organisation: ______

SUMMARY (Facts Only)

ACTIONS PROPOSED BY THEM:

FOLLOW-UP REQUIRED BY ME:

DEADLINE: ______

SECTION 3 – COMMUNICATION LOG

Incident Summary (Facts Only)

Who / What / When / Where / How

Keep it factual. *(Paste a copy of incident report if available)*

Date: ______

Time: ______

Method: ☐ Phone ☐ Email ☐ In Person ☐ Letter

Contact Person: ______

Organisation: ______

SUMMARY (Facts Only)

ACTIONS PROPOSED BY THEM:

FOLLOW-UP REQUIRED BY ME:

DEADLINE: ______

SECTION 3 – COMMUNICATION LOG

Incident Summary (Facts Only)

Who / What / When / Where / How

Keep it factual. *(Paste a copy of incident report if available)*

Date: ______

Time: ______

Method: ☐ Phone ☐ Email ☐ In Person ☐ Letter

Contact Person: ______

Organisation: ______

SUMMARY (Facts Only)

ACTIONS PROPOSED BY THEM:

FOLLOW-UP REQUIRED BY ME:

DEADLINE: ______

SECTION 3 – COMMUNICATION LOG

Incident Summary (Facts Only)

Who / What / When / Where / How

Keep it factual. *(Paste a copy of incident report if available)*

Date: ______

Time: ______

Method: ☐ Phone ☐ Email ☐ In Person ☐ Letter

Contact Person: ______

Organisation: ______

SUMMARY (Facts Only)

ACTIONS PROPOSED BY THEM:

FOLLOW-UP REQUIRED BY ME:

DEADLINE: ______

SECTION 3 – COMMUNICATION LOG

Incident Summary (Facts Only)

Who / What / When / Where / How

Keep it factual. *(Paste a copy of incident report if available)*

Date: ______

Time: ______

Method: ☐ Phone ☐ Email ☐ In Person ☐ Letter

Contact Person: ______

Organisation: ______

SUMMARY (Facts Only)

ACTIONS PROPOSED BY THEM:

FOLLOW-UP REQUIRED BY ME:

DEADLINE: ______

SECTION 3 – COMMUNICATION LOG

Incident Summary (Facts Only)

Who / What / When / Where / How

Keep it factual. *(Paste a copy of incident report if available)*

Date: ______________________

Time: ______________________

Method: ☐ Phone ☐ Email ☐ In Person ☐ Letter

Contact Person: ______________________

Organisation: ______________________

SUMMARY (Facts Only)

ACTIONS PROPOSED BY THEM:

FOLLOW-UP REQUIRED BY ME:

DEADLINE: ______________________

SECTION 3 – COMMUNICATION LOG

Incident Summary (Facts Only)

Who / What / When / Where / How

Keep it factual. *(Paste a copy of incident report if available)*

Date: ______________________

Time: ______________________

Method: ☐ Phone ☐ Email ☐ In Person ☐ Letter

Contact Person: ______________________

Organisation: ______________________

SUMMARY (Facts Only)

ACTIONS PROPOSED BY THEM:

FOLLOW-UP REQUIRED BY ME:

DEADLINE: ______________________

SECTION 3 – COMMUNICATION LOG

Incident Summary (Facts Only)

Who / What / When / Where / How

Keep it factual. *(Paste a copy of incident report if available)*

Date: ______________________

Time: ______________________

Method: ☐ Phone ☐ Email ☐ In Person ☐ Letter

Contact Person: ______________________

Organisation: ______________________

SUMMARY (Facts Only)

ACTIONS PROPOSED BY THEM:

FOLLOW-UP REQUIRED BY ME:

DEADLINE: ______________________

SECTION 3 – COMMUNICATION LOG

Incident Summary (Facts Only)

Who / What / When / Where / How

Keep it factual. *(Paste a copy of incident report if available)*

Date: ______________________

Time: ______________________

Method: ☐ Phone ☐ Email ☐ In Person ☐ Letter

Contact Person: ______________________

Organisation: ______________________

SUMMARY (Facts Only)

ACTIONS PROPOSED BY THEM:

FOLLOW-UP REQUIRED BY ME:

DEADLINE: ______________________

SECTION 3 – COMMUNICATION LOG

Incident Summary (Facts Only)

Who / What / When / Where / How

Keep it factual. *(Paste a copy of incident report if available)*

Date: ______

Time: ______

Method: ☐ Phone ☐ Email ☐ In Person ☐ Letter

Contact Person: ______

Organisation: ______

SUMMARY (Facts Only)

ACTIONS PROPOSED BY THEM:

FOLLOW-UP REQUIRED BY ME:

DEADLINE: ______

SECTION 3 – COMMUNICATION LOG

Incident Summary (Facts Only)

Who / What / When / Where / How

Keep it factual. *(Paste a copy of incident report if available)*

Date: ______

Time: ______

Method: ☐ Phone ☐ Email ☐ In Person ☐ Letter

Contact Person: ______

Organisation: ______

SUMMARY (Facts Only)

ACTIONS PROPOSED BY THEM:

FOLLOW-UP REQUIRED BY ME:

DEADLINE: ______

SECTION 3 – COMMUNICATION LOG

Incident Summary (Facts Only)

Who / What / When / Where / How

Keep it factual. *(Paste a copy of incident report if available)*

Date: ______

Time: ______

Method: ☐ Phone ☐ Email ☐ In Person ☐ Letter

Contact Person: ______

Organisation: ______

SUMMARY (Facts Only)

ACTIONS PROPOSED BY THEM:

FOLLOW-UP REQUIRED BY ME:

DEADLINE: ______

SECTION 3 – COMMUNICATION LOG

Incident Summary (Facts Only)

Who / What / When / Where / How

Keep it factual. *(Paste a copy of incident report if available)*

Date: ______

Time: ______

Method: ☐ Phone ☐ Email ☐ In Person ☐ Letter

Contact Person: ______

Organisation: ______

SUMMARY (Facts Only)

ACTIONS PROPOSED BY THEM:

FOLLOW-UP REQUIRED BY ME:

DEADLINE: ______

SECTION 3 – COMMUNICATION LOG

Incident Summary (Facts Only)

Who / What / When / Where / How

Keep it factual. *(Paste a copy of incident report if available)*

Date: ______

Time: ______

Method: ☐ Phone ☐ Email ☐ In Person ☐ Letter

Contact Person: ______

Organisation: ______

SUMMARY (Facts Only)

ACTIONS PROPOSED BY THEM:

FOLLOW-UP REQUIRED BY ME:

DEADLINE: ______

SECTION 3 – COMMUNICATION LOG

Incident Summary (Facts Only)

Who / What / When / Where / How

Keep it factual. *(Paste a copy of incident report if available)*

Date: ______

Time: ______

Method: ☐ Phone ☐ Email ☐ In Person ☐ Letter

Contact Person: ______

Organisation: ______

SUMMARY (Facts Only)

ACTIONS PROPOSED BY THEM:

FOLLOW-UP REQUIRED BY ME:

DEADLINE: ______

SECTION 3 – COMMUNICATION LOG

Incident Summary (Facts Only)

Who / What / When / Where / How

Keep it factual. *(Paste a copy of incident report if available)*

Date: ______

Time: ______

Method: ☐ Phone ☐ Email ☐ In Person ☐ Letter

Contact Person: ______

Organisation: ______

SUMMARY (Facts Only)

ACTIONS PROPOSED BY THEM:

FOLLOW-UP REQUIRED BY ME:

DEADLINE: ______

SECTION 3 – COMMUNICATION LOG

Incident Summary (Facts Only)

Who / What / When / Where / How

Keep it factual. *(Paste a copy of incident report if available)*

Date: ______

Time: ______

Method: ☐ Phone ☐ Email ☐ In Person ☐ Letter

Contact Person: ______

Organisation: ______

SUMMARY (Facts Only)

ACTIONS PROPOSED BY THEM:

FOLLOW-UP REQUIRED BY ME:

DEADLINE: ______

SECTION 3 – COMMUNICATION LOG

Incident Summary (Facts Only)

Who / What / When / Where / How

Keep it factual. *(Paste a copy of incident report if available)*

Date: ______________________

Time: ______________________

Method: ☐ Phone ☐ Email ☐ In Person ☐ Letter

Contact Person: ______________________

Organisation: ______________________

SUMMARY (Facts Only)

ACTIONS PROPOSED BY THEM:

FOLLOW-UP REQUIRED BY ME:

DEADLINE: ______________________

SECTION 3 – COMMUNICATION LOG

Incident Summary (Facts Only)

Who / What / When / Where / How

Keep it factual. *(Paste a copy of incident report if available)*

Date: ______________________

Time: ______________________

Method: ☐ Phone ☐ Email ☐ In Person ☐ Letter

Contact Person: ______________________

Organisation: ______________________

SUMMARY (Facts Only)

ACTIONS PROPOSED BY THEM:

FOLLOW-UP REQUIRED BY ME:

DEADLINE: ______________________

SECTION 3 – COMMUNICATION LOG

Incident Summary (Facts Only)

Who / What / When / Where / How

Keep it factual. *(Paste a copy of incident report if available)*

Date: ______________________

Time: ______________________

Method: ☐ Phone ☐ Email ☐ In Person ☐ Letter

Contact Person: ______________________

Organisation: ______________________

SUMMARY (Facts Only)

ACTIONS PROPOSED BY THEM:

FOLLOW-UP REQUIRED BY ME:

DEADLINE: ______________________

SECTION 3 – COMMUNICATION LOG

Incident Summary (Facts Only)

Who / What / When / Where / How

Keep it factual. *(Paste a copy of incident report if available)*

Date: ______________________

Time: ______________________

Method: ☐ Phone ☐ Email ☐ In Person ☐ Letter

Contact Person: ______________________

Organisation: ______________________

SUMMARY (Facts Only)

ACTIONS PROPOSED BY THEM:

FOLLOW-UP REQUIRED BY ME:

DEADLINE: ______________________

SECTION 3 – COMMUNICATION LOG

Incident Summary (Facts Only)

Who / What / When / Where / How

Keep it factual. *(Paste a copy of incident report if available)*

Date: ______________________

Time: ______________________

Method: ☐ Phone ☐ Email ☐ In Person ☐ Letter

Contact Person: ______________________

Organisation: ______________________

SUMMARY (Facts Only)

ACTIONS PROPOSED BY THEM:

FOLLOW-UP REQUIRED BY ME:

SECTION 3 – COMMUNICATION LOG

Incident Summary (Facts Only)

Who / What / When / Where / How

Keep it factual. *(Paste a copy of incident report if available)*

Date: ______________________

Time: ______________________

Method: ☐ Phone ☐ Email ☐ In Person ☐ Letter

Contact Person: ______________________

Organisation: ______________________

SUMMARY (Facts Only)

ACTIONS PROPOSED BY THEM:

FOLLOW-UP REQUIRED BY ME:

SECTION 3 – COMMUNICATION LOG

Incident Summary (Facts Only)

Who / What / When / Where / How

Keep it factual. *(Paste a copy of incident report if available)*

Date: ______________________

Time: ______________________

Method: ☐ Phone ☐ Email ☐ In Person ☐ Letter

Contact Person: ______________________

Organisation: ______________________

SUMMARY (Facts Only)

ACTIONS PROPOSED BY THEM:

FOLLOW-UP REQUIRED BY ME:

DEADLINE: ______________________

SECTION 3 – COMMUNICATION LOG

Incident Summary (Facts Only)

Who / What / When / Where / How

Keep it factual. *(Paste a copy of incident report if available)*

Date: ______________________

Time: ______________________

Method: ☐ Phone ☐ Email ☐ In Person ☐ Letter

Contact Person: ______________________

Organisation: ______________________

SUMMARY (Facts Only)

ACTIONS PROPOSED BY THEM:

FOLLOW-UP REQUIRED BY ME:

DEADLINE: ______________________

SECTION 3 – COMMUNICATION LOG

Incident Summary (Facts Only)
Who / What / When / Where / How

Keep it factual. *(Paste a copy of incident report if available)*

Date: ____________________

Time: ____________________

Method: ☐ Phone ☐ Email ☐ In Person ☐ Letter

Contact Person: ____________________

Organisation: ____________________

SUMMARY (Facts Only)

ACTIONS PROPOSED BY THEM:

FOLLOW-UP REQUIRED BY ME:

DEADLINE: ____________________

SECTION 3 – COMMUNICATION LOG

Incident Summary (Facts Only)
Who / What / When / Where / How

Keep it factual. *(Paste a copy of incident report if available)*

Date: ____________________

Time: ____________________

Method: ☐ Phone ☐ Email ☐ In Person ☐ Letter

Contact Person: ____________________

Organisation: ____________________

SUMMARY (Facts Only)

ACTIONS PROPOSED BY THEM:

FOLLOW-UP REQUIRED BY ME:

DEADLINE: ____________________

SECTION 3 – COMMUNICATION LOG

Incident Summary (Facts Only)
Who / What / When / Where / How

Keep it factual. *(Paste a copy of incident report if available)*

Date: ____________________

Time: ____________________

Method: ☐ Phone ☐ Email ☐ In Person ☐ Letter

Contact Person: ____________________

Organisation: ____________________

SUMMARY (Facts Only)

ACTIONS PROPOSED BY THEM:

FOLLOW-UP REQUIRED BY ME:

DEADLINE: ____________________

SECTION 3 – COMMUNICATION LOG

Incident Summary (Facts Only)
Who / What / When / Where / How

Keep it factual. *(Paste a copy of incident report if available)*

Date: ____________________

Time: ____________________

Method: ☐ Phone ☐ Email ☐ In Person ☐ Letter

Contact Person: ____________________

Organisation: ____________________

SUMMARY (Facts Only)

ACTIONS PROPOSED BY THEM:

FOLLOW-UP REQUIRED BY ME:

DEADLINE: ____________________

SECTION 3 – COMMUNICATION LOG

Incident Summary (Facts Only)

Who / What / When / Where / How

Keep it factual. *(Paste a copy of incident report if available)*

Date: ____

Time: ____

Method: ☐ Phone ☐ Email ☐ In Person ☐ Letter

Contact Person: ____

Organisation: ____

SUMMARY (Facts Only)

ACTIONS PROPOSED BY THEM:

FOLLOW-UP REQUIRED BY ME:

DEADLINE: ____

SECTION 3 – COMMUNICATION LOG

Incident Summary (Facts Only)

Who / What / When / Where / How

Keep it factual. *(Paste a copy of incident report if available)*

Date: ____

Time: ____

Method: ☐ Phone ☐ Email ☐ In Person ☐ Letter

Contact Person: ____

Organisation: ____

SUMMARY (Facts Only)

ACTIONS PROPOSED BY THEM:

FOLLOW-UP REQUIRED BY ME:

DEADLINE: ____

SECTION 3 – COMMUNICATION LOG

Incident Summary (Facts Only)

Who / What / When / Where / How

Keep it factual. *(Paste a copy of incident report if available)*

Date: ____

Time: ____

Method: ☐ Phone ☐ Email ☐ In Person ☐ Letter

Contact Person: ____

Organisation: ____

SUMMARY (Facts Only)

ACTIONS PROPOSED BY THEM:

FOLLOW-UP REQUIRED BY ME:

DEADLINE: ____

SECTION 3 – COMMUNICATION LOG

Incident Summary (Facts Only)

Who / What / When / Where / How

Keep it factual. *(Paste a copy of incident report if available)*

Date: ____

Time: ____

Method: ☐ Phone ☐ Email ☐ In Person ☐ Letter

Contact Person: ____

Organisation: ____

SUMMARY (Facts Only)

ACTIONS PROPOSED BY THEM:

FOLLOW-UP REQUIRED BY ME:

DEADLINE: ____

SECTION 3 – COMMUNICATION LOG

Incident Summary (Facts Only)

Who / What / When / Where / How

Keep it factual. *(Paste a copy of incident report if available)*

Date: ____________________

Time: ____________________

Method: ☐ Phone ☐ Email ☐ In Person ☐ Letter

Contact Person: ____________________

Organisation: ____________________

SUMMARY (Facts Only)

ACTIONS PROPOSED BY THEM:

FOLLOW-UP REQUIRED BY ME:

DEADLINE: ____________________

SECTION 3 – COMMUNICATION LOG

Incident Summary (Facts Only)

Who / What / When / Where / How

Keep it factual. *(Paste a copy of incident report if available)*

Date: ____________________

Time: ____________________

Method: ☐ Phone ☐ Email ☐ In Person ☐ Letter

Contact Person: ____________________

Organisation: ____________________

SUMMARY (Facts Only)

ACTIONS PROPOSED BY THEM:

FOLLOW-UP REQUIRED BY ME:

DEADLINE: ____________________

SECTION 3 – COMMUNICATION LOG

Incident Summary (Facts Only)

Who / What / When / Where / How

Keep it factual. *(Paste a copy of incident report if available)*

Date: ____________________

Time: ____________________

Method: ☐ Phone ☐ Email ☐ In Person ☐ Letter

Contact Person: ____________________

Organisation: ____________________

SUMMARY (Facts Only)

ACTIONS PROPOSED BY THEM:

FOLLOW-UP REQUIRED BY ME:

DEADLINE: ____________________

SECTION 3 – COMMUNICATION LOG

Incident Summary (Facts Only)

Who / What / When / Where / How

Keep it factual. *(Paste a copy of incident report if available)*

Date: ____________________

Time: ____________________

Method: ☐ Phone ☐ Email ☐ In Person ☐ Letter

Contact Person: ____________________

Organisation: ____________________

SUMMARY (Facts Only)

ACTIONS PROPOSED BY THEM:

FOLLOW-UP REQUIRED BY ME:

DEADLINE: ____________________

SECTION 3 – COMMUNICATION LOG

Incident Summary (Facts Only)

Who / What / When / Where / How

Keep it factual. *(Paste a copy of incident report if available)*

Date: ______________________

Time: ______________________

Method: ☐ Phone ☐ Email ☐ In Person ☐ Letter

Contact Person: ______________________

Organisation: ______________________

SUMMARY (Facts Only)

ACTIONS PROPOSED BY THEM:

FOLLOW-UP REQUIRED BY ME:

DEADLINE: ______________________

SECTION 3 – COMMUNICATION LOG

Incident Summary (Facts Only)

Who / What / When / Where / How

Keep it factual. *(Paste a copy of incident report if available)*

Date: ______________________

Time: ______________________

Method: ☐ Phone ☐ Email ☐ In Person ☐ Letter

Contact Person: ______________________

Organisation: ______________________

SUMMARY (Facts Only)

ACTIONS PROPOSED BY THEM:

FOLLOW-UP REQUIRED BY ME:

DEADLINE: ______________________

SECTION 3 – COMMUNICATION LOG

Incident Summary (Facts Only)

Who / What / When / Where / How

Keep it factual. *(Paste a copy of incident report if available)*

Date: ______________________

Time: ______________________

Method: ☐ Phone ☐ Email ☐ In Person ☐ Letter

Contact Person: ______________________

Organisation: ______________________

SUMMARY (Facts Only)

ACTIONS PROPOSED BY THEM:

FOLLOW-UP REQUIRED BY ME:

DEADLINE: ______________________

SECTION 3 – COMMUNICATION LOG

Incident Summary (Facts Only)

Who / What / When / Where / How

Keep it factual. *(Paste a copy of incident report if available)*

Date: ______________________

Time: ______________________

Method: ☐ Phone ☐ Email ☐ In Person ☐ Letter

Contact Person: ______________________

Organisation: ______________________

SUMMARY (Facts Only)

ACTIONS PROPOSED BY THEM:

FOLLOW-UP REQUIRED BY ME:

DEADLINE: ______________________

SECTION 3 – COMMUNICATION LOG

Incident Summary (Facts Only)

Who / What / When / Where / How

Keep it factual. *(Paste a copy of incident report if available)*

Date: ____________________

Time: ____________________

Method: ☐ Phone ☐ Email ☐ In Person ☐ Letter

Contact Person: ____________________

Organisation: ____________________

SUMMARY (Facts Only)

ACTIONS PROPOSED BY THEM:

FOLLOW-UP REQUIRED BY ME:

DEADLINE: ____________________

SECTION 3 – COMMUNICATION LOG

Incident Summary (Facts Only)

Who / What / When / Where / How

Keep it factual. *(Paste a copy of incident report if available)*

Date: ____________________

Time: ____________________

Method: ☐ Phone ☐ Email ☐ In Person ☐ Letter

Contact Person: ____________________

Organisation: ____________________

SUMMARY (Facts Only)

ACTIONS PROPOSED BY THEM:

FOLLOW-UP REQUIRED BY ME:

DEADLINE: ____________________

SECTION 3 – COMMUNICATION LOG

Incident Summary (Facts Only)

Who / What / When / Where / How

Keep it factual. *(Paste a copy of incident report if available)*

Date: ____________________

Time: ____________________

Method: ☐ Phone ☐ Email ☐ In Person ☐ Letter

Contact Person: ____________________

Organisation: ____________________

SUMMARY (Facts Only)

ACTIONS PROPOSED BY THEM:

FOLLOW-UP REQUIRED BY ME:

DEADLINE: ____________________

SECTION 3 – COMMUNICATION LOG

Incident Summary (Facts Only)

Who / What / When / Where / How

Keep it factual. *(Paste a copy of incident report if available)*

Date: ____________________

Time: ____________________

Method: ☐ Phone ☐ Email ☐ In Person ☐ Letter

Contact Person: ____________________

Organisation: ____________________

SUMMARY (Facts Only)

ACTIONS PROPOSED BY THEM:

FOLLOW-UP REQUIRED BY ME:

DEADLINE: ____________________

SECTION 3 – COMMUNICATION LOG

Incident Summary (Facts Only)
Who / What / When / Where / How
Keep it factual. *(Paste a copy of incident report if available)*

Date: ______
Time: ______
Method: ☐ Phone ☐ Email ☐ In Person ☐ Letter
Contact Person: ______
Organisation: ______

SUMMARY (Facts Only)

ACTIONS PROPOSED BY THEM:

FOLLOW-UP REQUIRED BY ME:

DEADLINE: ______

SECTION 3 – COMMUNICATION LOG

Incident Summary (Facts Only)
Who / What / When / Where / How
Keep it factual. *(Paste a copy of incident report if available)*

Date: ______
Time: ______
Method: ☐ Phone ☐ Email ☐ In Person ☐ Letter
Contact Person: ______
Organisation: ______

SUMMARY (Facts Only)

ACTIONS PROPOSED BY THEM:

FOLLOW-UP REQUIRED BY ME:

DEADLINE: ______

SECTION 3 – COMMUNICATION LOG

Incident Summary (Facts Only)
Who / What / When / Where / How
Keep it factual. *(Paste a copy of incident report if available)*

Date: ______
Time: ______
Method: ☐ Phone ☐ Email ☐ In Person ☐ Letter
Contact Person: ______
Organisation: ______

SUMMARY (Facts Only)

ACTIONS PROPOSED BY THEM:

FOLLOW-UP REQUIRED BY ME:

DEADLINE: ______

SECTION 3 – COMMUNICATION LOG

Incident Summary (Facts Only)
Who / What / When / Where / How
Keep it factual. *(Paste a copy of incident report if available)*

Date: ______
Time: ______
Method: ☐ Phone ☐ Email ☐ In Person ☐ Letter
Contact Person: ______
Organisation: ______

SUMMARY (Facts Only)

ACTIONS PROPOSED BY THEM:

FOLLOW-UP REQUIRED BY ME:

DEADLINE: ______

SECTION 3 – COMMUNICATION LOG

Incident Summary (Facts Only)
Who / What / When / Where / How
Keep it factual. *(Paste a copy of incident report if available)*

Date: ______________________
Time: ______________________
Method: ☐ Phone ☐ Email ☐ In Person ☐ Letter
Contact Person: ______________________
Organisation: ______________________

SUMMARY (Facts Only)

ACTIONS PROPOSED BY THEM:

FOLLOW-UP REQUIRED BY ME:

DEADLINE: ______________________

SECTION 3 – COMMUNICATION LOG

Incident Summary (Facts Only)
Who / What / When / Where / How
Keep it factual. *(Paste a copy of incident report if available)*

Date: ______________________
Time: ______________________
Method: ☐ Phone ☐ Email ☐ In Person ☐ Letter
Contact Person: ______________________
Organisation: ______________________

SUMMARY (Facts Only)

ACTIONS PROPOSED BY THEM:

FOLLOW-UP REQUIRED BY ME:

DEADLINE: ______________________

SECTION 3 – COMMUNICATION LOG

Incident Summary (Facts Only)
Who / What / When / Where / How
Keep it factual. *(Paste a copy of incident report if available)*

Date: ______________________
Time: ______________________
Method: ☐ Phone ☐ Email ☐ In Person ☐ Letter
Contact Person: ______________________
Organisation: ______________________

SUMMARY (Facts Only)

ACTIONS PROPOSED BY THEM:

FOLLOW-UP REQUIRED BY ME:

DEADLINE: ______________________

SECTION 3 – COMMUNICATION LOG

Incident Summary (Facts Only)
Who / What / When / Where / How
Keep it factual. *(Paste a copy of incident report if available)*

Date: ______________________
Time: ______________________
Method: ☐ Phone ☐ Email ☐ In Person ☐ Letter
Contact Person: ______________________
Organisation: ______________________

SUMMARY (Facts Only)

ACTIONS PROPOSED BY THEM:

FOLLOW-UP REQUIRED BY ME:

DEADLINE: ______________________

SECTION 3 – COMMUNICATION LOG

Incident Summary (Facts Only)

Who / What / When / Where / How

Keep it factual. *(Paste a copy of incident report if available)*

Date: ______

Time: ______

Method: ☐ Phone ☐ Email ☐ In Person ☐ Letter

Contact Person: ______

Organisation: ______

SUMMARY (Facts Only)

ACTIONS PROPOSED BY THEM:

FOLLOW-UP REQUIRED BY ME:

DEADLINE: ______

SECTION 3 – COMMUNICATION LOG

Incident Summary (Facts Only)

Who / What / When / Where / How

Keep it factual. *(Paste a copy of incident report if available)*

Date: ______

Time: ______

Method: ☐ Phone ☐ Email ☐ In Person ☐ Letter

Contact Person: ______

Organisation: ______

SUMMARY (Facts Only)

ACTIONS PROPOSED BY THEM:

FOLLOW-UP REQUIRED BY ME:

DEADLINE: ______

SECTION 3 – COMMUNICATION LOG

Incident Summary (Facts Only)

Who / What / When / Where / How

Keep it factual. *(Paste a copy of incident report if available)*

Date: ______

Time: ______

Method: ☐ Phone ☐ Email ☐ In Person ☐ Letter

Contact Person: ______

Organisation: ______

SUMMARY (Facts Only)

ACTIONS PROPOSED BY THEM:

FOLLOW-UP REQUIRED BY ME:

DEADLINE: ______

SECTION 3 – COMMUNICATION LOG

Incident Summary (Facts Only)

Who / What / When / Where / How

Keep it factual. *(Paste a copy of incident report if available)*

Date: ______

Time: ______

Method: ☐ Phone ☐ Email ☐ In Person ☐ Letter

Contact Person: ______

Organisation: ______

SUMMARY (Facts Only)

ACTIONS PROPOSED BY THEM:

FOLLOW-UP REQUIRED BY ME:

DEADLINE: ______

SECTION 3 – COMMUNICATION LOG

Incident Summary (Facts Only)
Who / What / When / Where / How

Keep it factual. *(Paste a copy of incident report if available)*

Date: ______________________
Time: ______________________
Method: ☐ Phone ☐ Email ☐ In Person ☐ Letter
Contact Person: ______________________
Organisation: ______________________

SUMMARY (Facts Only)

ACTIONS PROPOSED BY THEM:

FOLLOW-UP REQUIRED BY ME:

DEADLINE: ______________________

SECTION 3 – COMMUNICATION LOG

Incident Summary (Facts Only)
Who / What / When / Where / How

Keep it factual. *(Paste a copy of incident report if available)*

Date: ______________________
Time: ______________________
Method: ☐ Phone ☐ Email ☐ In Person ☐ Letter
Contact Person: ______________________
Organisation: ______________________

SUMMARY (Facts Only)

ACTIONS PROPOSED BY THEM:

FOLLOW-UP REQUIRED BY ME:

DEADLINE: ______________________

SECTION 3 – COMMUNICATION LOG

Incident Summary (Facts Only)
Who / What / When / Where / How

Keep it factual. *(Paste a copy of incident report if available)*

Date: ______________________
Time: ______________________
Method: ☐ Phone ☐ Email ☐ In Person ☐ Letter
Contact Person: ______________________
Organisation: ______________________

SUMMARY (Facts Only)

ACTIONS PROPOSED BY THEM:

FOLLOW-UP REQUIRED BY ME:

DEADLINE: ______________________

SECTION 3 – COMMUNICATION LOG

Incident Summary (Facts Only)
Who / What / When / Where / How

Keep it factual. *(Paste a copy of incident report if available)*

Date: ______________________
Time: ______________________
Method: ☐ Phone ☐ Email ☐ In Person ☐ Letter
Contact Person: ______________________
Organisation: ______________________

SUMMARY (Facts Only)

ACTIONS PROPOSED BY THEM:

FOLLOW-UP REQUIRED BY ME:

DEADLINE: ______________________

SECTION 4 – MEDICAL & APPOINTMENT LOG

Date: ____________________ Provider: ____________________

Specialty: ____________________

Reason for Visit:

Key Findings / Diagnosis:

Recommendations / Medication:

Capacity Status: ☐ Pre-injury duties ☐ *Suitable / modified duties* ☐ *No capacity*

Follow-up Date: ____________________

CHECKLIST:

☐ Certificate issued

☐ Report requested

☐ Report received

☐ Submitted to insurer

OTHER NOTES:

SECTION 4 – MEDICAL & APPOINTMENT LOG

Date: ____________________ Provider: ____________________

Specialty: ____________________

Reason for Visit:

Key Findings / Diagnosis:

Recommendations / Medication:

Capacity Status: ☐ Pre-injury duties ☐ *Suitable / modified duties* ☐ *No capacity*

Follow-up Date: ____________________

CHECKLIST:

☐ Certificate issued

☐ Report requested

☐ Report received

☐ Submitted to insurer

OTHER NOTES:

SECTION 4 – MEDICAL & APPOINTMENT LOG

Date: ____________________ Provider: ____________________

Specialty: ____________________

Reason for Visit:

Key Findings / Diagnosis:

Recommendations / Medication:

Capacity Status: ☐ Pre-injury duties ☐ *Suitable / modified duties* ☐ *No capacity*

Follow-up Date: ____________________

CHECKLIST:

☐ Certificate issued

☐ Report requested

☐ Report received

☐ Submitted to insurer

OTHER NOTES:

SECTION 4 – MEDICAL & APPOINTMENT LOG

Date: ____________________ Provider: ____________________

Specialty: ____________________

Reason for Visit:

Key Findings / Diagnosis:

Recommendations / Medication:

Capacity Status: ☐ Pre-injury duties ☐ *Suitable / modified duties* ☐ *No capacity*

Follow-up Date: ____________________

CHECKLIST:

☐ Certificate issued

☐ Report requested

☐ Report received

☐ Submitted to insurer

OTHER NOTES:

SECTION 4 – **MEDICAL & APPOINTMENT LOG**

Date: ______________________ Provider: ______________________
Specialty: ______________________

Reason for Visit:

Key Findings / Diagnosis:

Recommendations / Medication:

Capacity Status: ☐ Pre-injury duties ☐ *Suitable / modified duties* ☐ *No capacity*
Follow-up Date: ______________________

CHECKLIST:

☐ Certificate issued
☐ Report requested
☐ Report received
☐ Submitted to insurer

OTHER NOTES:

SECTION 4 – **MEDICAL & APPOINTMENT LOG**

Date: ______________________ Provider: ______________________
Specialty: ______________________

Reason for Visit:

Key Findings / Diagnosis:

Recommendations / Medication:

Capacity Status: ☐ Pre-injury duties ☐ *Suitable / modified duties* ☐ *No capacity*
Follow-up Date: ______________________

CHECKLIST:

☐ Certificate issued
☐ Report requested
☐ Report received
☐ Submitted to insurer

OTHER NOTES:

SECTION 4 – **MEDICAL & APPOINTMENT LOG**

Date: ______________________ Provider: ______________________
Specialty: ______________________

Reason for Visit:

Key Findings / Diagnosis:

Recommendations / Medication:

Capacity Status: ☐ Pre-injury duties ☐ *Suitable / modified duties* ☐ *No capacity*
Follow-up Date: ______________________

CHECKLIST:

☐ Certificate issued
☐ Report requested
☐ Report received
☐ Submitted to insurer

OTHER NOTES:

SECTION 4 – **MEDICAL & APPOINTMENT LOG**

Date: ______________________ Provider: ______________________
Specialty: ______________________

Reason for Visit:

Key Findings / Diagnosis:

Recommendations / Medication:

Capacity Status: ☐ Pre-injury duties ☐ *Suitable / modified duties* ☐ *No capacity*
Follow-up Date: ______________________

CHECKLIST:

☐ Certificate issued
☐ Report requested
☐ Report received
☐ Submitted to insurer

OTHER NOTES:

SECTION 4 – **MEDICAL & APPOINTMENT LOG**

Date: ______________ Provider: ______________

Specialty: ______________

Reason for Visit:

Key Findings / Diagnosis:

Recommendations / Medication:

Capacity Status: ☐ Pre-injury duties ☐ *Suitable / modified duties* ☐ *No capacity*

Follow-up Date: ______________

CHECKLIST:

☐ Certificate issued ______________

☐ Report requested ______________

☐ Report received ______________

☐ Submitted to insurer ______________

OTHER NOTES:

SECTION 4 – **MEDICAL & APPOINTMENT LOG**

Date: ______________ Provider: ______________

Specialty: ______________

Reason for Visit:

Key Findings / Diagnosis:

Recommendations / Medication:

Capacity Status: ☐ Pre-injury duties ☐ *Suitable / modified duties* ☐ *No capacity*

Follow-up Date: ______________

CHECKLIST:

☐ Certificate issued ______________

☐ Report requested ______________

☐ Report received ______________

☐ Submitted to insurer ______________

OTHER NOTES:

SECTION 4 – **MEDICAL & APPOINTMENT LOG**

Date: ______________ Provider: ______________

Specialty: ______________

Reason for Visit:

Key Findings / Diagnosis:

Recommendations / Medication:

Capacity Status: ☐ Pre-injury duties ☐ *Suitable / modified duties* ☐ *No capacity*

Follow-up Date: ______________

CHECKLIST:

☐ Certificate issued ______________

☐ Report requested ______________

☐ Report received ______________

☐ Submitted to insurer ______________

OTHER NOTES:

SECTION 4 – **MEDICAL & APPOINTMENT LOG**

Date: ______________ Provider: ______________

Specialty: ______________

Reason for Visit:

Key Findings / Diagnosis:

Recommendations / Medication:

Capacity Status: ☐ Pre-injury duties ☐ *Suitable / modified duties* ☐ *No capacity*

Follow-up Date: ______________

CHECKLIST:

☐ Certificate issued ______________

☐ Report requested ______________

☐ Report received ______________

☐ Submitted to insurer ______________

OTHER NOTES:

Appointment & Medical Report Tracker

Insurance and compensation claims often rely heavily on medical reports.
Over time, claimants may see multiple doctors, specialists, and treatment providers.

It can become difficult to remember:

- which doctor diagnosed the injury
- when treatment began
- whether reports were sent to the insurer
- which specialist provided key opinions

This page provides a simple overview of medical appointments and reports to help track the medical evidence in your claim.

- GP
- Psychologist
- Psychiatrist
- Physiotherapist
- Specialist Surgeon
- Pain Specialist
- Occupational Therapist
- Rehabilitation Provider
- Independent Medical Examiner (IME)

Date	Doctor / Specialist	Provider Type	Reason for Appointm	Report Sent to Insurer	Notes
				☐ Yes ☐ No	
				☐ Yes ☐ No	
				☐ Yes ☐ No	
				☐ Yes ☐ No	
				☐ Yes ☐ No	
				☐ Yes ☐ No	
				☐ Yes ☐ No	

SECTION 5 – EVIDENCE REGISTER

Claim Reference: ______________________________

Date Added: ______________ Date Submitted: ______________

Evidence Type: ______________________________

Description / Details:

Submitted To: ______________________ Receipt Confirmed: Yes ■ No ■

Location Stored / File Reference: ______________________________

Date Added: ______________ Date Submitted: ______________

Evidence Type: ______________________________

Description / Details:

Submitted To: ______________________ Receipt Confirmed: Yes ■ No ■

Location Stored / File Reference: ______________________________

Date Added: ______________ Date Submitted: ______________

Evidence Type: ______________________________

Description / Details:

Submitted To: ______________________ Receipt Confirmed: Yes ■ No ■

Location Stored / File Reference: ______________________________

Date Added: ______________ Date Submitted: ______________

Evidence Type: ______________________________

Description / Details:

Submitted To: ______________________ Receipt Confirmed: Yes ■ No ■

Location Stored / File Reference: ______________________________

Date Added: ______________ Date Submitted: ______________

Evidence Type: ______________________________

Description / Details:

Submitted To: ______________________ Receipt Confirmed: Yes ■ No ■

Location Stored / File Reference: ______________________________

Date Added: ______________ Date Submitted: ______________

Evidence Type: ______________________________

Description / Details:

SECTION 5 – MEDICAL EVIDENCE REGISTER

Claim Reference:____

Date Added: ______________________ Date Submitted: ______________________

Evidence Type: ____

Description / Details:

____

____

Submitted To: ___________________________________ Receipt Confirmed: Yes ▪ No ▪

Location Stored / File Reference: ____

Date Added: ______________________ Date Submitted: ______________________

Evidence Type: ____

Description / Details:

____

____

Submitted To: ___________________________________ Receipt Confirmed: Yes ▪ No ▪

Location Stored / File Reference: ____

Date Added: ______________________ Date Submitted: ______________________

Evidence Type: ____

Description / Details:

____

____

Submitted To: ___________________________________ Receipt Confirmed: Yes ▪ No ▪

Location Stored / File Reference: ____

Date Added: ______________________ Date Submitted: ______________________

Evidence Type: ____

Description / Details:

____

____

Submitted To: ___________________________________ Receipt Confirmed: Yes ▪ No ▪

Location Stored / File Reference: ____

Date Added: ______________________ Date Submitted: ______________________

Evidence Type: ____

Description / Details:

____

____

Submitted To: ___________________________________ Receipt Confirmed: Yes ▪ No ▪

Location Stored / File Reference: ____

Date Added: ______________________ Date Submitted: ______________________

Evidence Type: ____

Description / Details:

____

SECTION 5 – EVIDENCE REGISTER

Claim Reference:____

Date Added: _____________________ Date Submitted: _____________________

Evidence Type: ____

Description / Details:

____

____

Submitted To: __________________________________ Receipt Confirmed: Yes ▪ No ▪

Location Stored / File Reference: ____

____

Date Added: _____________________ Date Submitted: _____________________

Evidence Type: ____

Description / Details:

____

____

Submitted To: __________________________________ Receipt Confirmed: Yes ▪ No ▪

Location Stored / File Reference: ____

____

Date Added: _____________________ Date Submitted: _____________________

Evidence Type: ____

Description / Details:

____

____

Submitted To: __________________________________ Receipt Confirmed: Yes ▪ No ▪

Location Stored / File Reference: ____

____

Date Added: _____________________ Date Submitted: _____________________

Evidence Type: ____

Description / Details:

____

____

Submitted To: __________________________________ Receipt Confirmed: Yes ▪ No ▪

Location Stored / File Reference: ____

____

Date Added: _____________________ Date Submitted: _____________________

Evidence Type: ____

Description / Details:

____

____

Submitted To: __________________________________ Receipt Confirmed: Yes ▪ No ▪

Location Stored / File Reference: ____

____

Date Added: _____________________ Date Submitted: _____________________

Evidence Type: ____

Description / Details:

____

SECTION 6 – FINANCIAL & REIMBURSEMENT TRACKER

Expense Log

Date Incurred	Date Submitted	Provider / Expense Description	Category	Amount ($)	Submitted to Insurer	Paid	Out-Standing
				☐ Yes ☐ No	☐ Yes ☐ No	☐ Yes ☐ No	☐ Yes ☐ No

Category: ______________________ **Totals:** ______________

☐ Medication ☐ GP ☐ Specialist ☐ Arms ☐ Leg

☐ Physio ☐ Psychogey ☐ Travel ☐ Equipment ☐ Other: ____

Functional Limits Today:

☐ Driving ☐ Standing ☐ Sitting ☐ Lifting ☐ Household tasks

☐ Work duties ______________________ ☐ Other: ______

Work Impact Today:

____

Brief Daily Note (1-2 sentences):

____

____

Page Total: $ ______________________

Running Total Outstanding: $ ____________

SECTION 6 – FINANCIAL & REIMBURSEMENT TRACKER

Expense Log

Date Incurred	Date Submitted	Provider / Expense Description	Category	Amount ($)	Submitted to Insurer	Paid	Out-Standing
				☐ Yes ☐ No	☐ Yes ☐ No	☐ Yes ☐ No	☐ Yes ☐ No

Category: ____________________ **Totals:** ____________________

☐ Medication ☐ GP ☐ Specialist ☐ Arms ☐ Leg

☐ Physio ☐ Psychogey ☐ Travel ☐ Equipment ☐ Other: ____

Functional Limits Today:

☐ Driving ☐ Standing ☐ Sitting ☐ Lifting ☐ Household tasks

☐ Work duties ____________________ ☐ Other: ____________

Work Impact Today:

____

Brief Daily Note (1-2 sentences):

____

____

Page Total: $ ____________________

Running Total Outstanding: $ ____________

SECTION 6 – FINANCIAL & REIMBURSEMENT TRACKER

Expense Log

Date Incurred	Date Submitted	Provider / Expense Description	Category	Amount ($)	Submitted to Insurer	Paid	Out-Standing
				☐ Yes ☐ No	☐ Yes ☐ No	☐ Yes ☐ No	☐ Yes ☐ No

Category: ____________________ **Totals:** ________________

☐ Medication ☐ GP ☐ Specialist ☐ Arms ☐ Leg

☐ Physio ☐ Psychogey ☐ Travel ☐ Equipment ☐ Other: ____

Functional Limits Today:

☐ Driving ☐ Standing ☐ Sitting ☐ Lifting ☐ Household tasks

☐ Work duties ________________________ ☐ Other: __________

Work Impact Today:

____

Brief Daily Note (1-2 sentences):

____

____

Page Total: $ ______________________

Running Total Outstanding: $ __________

SECTION 6 – FINANCIAL & REIMBURSEMENT TRACKER

Date Incurred	Date Submitted	Provider / Expense Description	Amount ($)	Submitted to Insurer	Approved	Paid	Outstanding
				☐ Yes ☐ No	☐ Yes ☐ No	☐ Yes ☐ No	☐ Yes ☐ No
				☐ Yes ☐ No	☐ Yes ☐ No	☐ Yes ☐ No	☐ Yes ☐ No
				☐ Yes ☐ No	☐ Yes ☐ No	☐ Yes ☐ No	☐ Yes ☐ No
				☐ Yes ☐ No	☐ Yes ☐ No	☐ Yes ☐ No	☐ Yes ☐ No
				☐ Yes ☐ No	☐ Yes ☐ No	☐ Yes ☐ No	☐ Yes ☐ No
				☐ Yes ☐ No	☐ Yes ☐ No	☐ Yes ☐ No	☐ Yes ☐ No
				☐ Yes ☐ No	☐ Yes ☐ No	☐ Yes ☐ No	☐ Yes ☐ No
				☐ Yes ☐ No	☐ Yes ☐ No	☐ Yes ☐ No	☐ Yes ☐ No
				☐ Yes ☐ No	☐ Yes ☐ No	☐ Yes ☐ No	☐ Yes ☐ No
				☐ Yes ☐ No	☐ Yes ☐ No	☐ Yes ☐ No	☐ Yes ☐ No
				☐ Yes ☐ No	☐ Yes ☐ No	☐ Yes ☐ No	☐ Yes ☐ No
				☐ Yes ☐ No	☐ Yes ☐ No	☐ Yes ☐ No	☐ Yes ☐ No
				☐ Yes ☐ No	☐ Yes ☐ No	☐ Yes ☐ No	☐ Yes ☐ No
				☐ Yes ☐ No	☐ Yes ☐ No	☐ Yes ☐ No	☐ Yes ☐ No
				☐ Yes ☐ No	☐ Yes ☐ No	☐ Yes ☐ No	☐ Yes ☐ No
				☐ Yes ☐ No	☐ Yes ☐ No	☐ Yes ☐ No	☐ Yes ☐ No
				☐ Yes ☐ No	☐ Yes ☐ No	☐ Yes ☐ No	☐ Yes ☐ No

SECTION 7 – MEDICAL RECORDS & REPORTS LOG

Expense Log

Date Received	Document Type	Provider / Specialist	Document Name	Pages	Submitted to Insurer	Notes	Confirm Received?
					☐ Yes ☐ No	☐ Yes ☐ No	☐ Yes ☐ No

Total Pages Received: ____________________

Documents Submitted to Insurer: ☐ / ______

Documents Confirmed Received: ☐ / ______

KEY FOLLOW-UP NOTES:

☐ Medication ☐ GP ☐ Specialist ☐ Arms ☐ Leg

☐ Physio ☐ Psychology ☐ Travel ☐ Equipment ☐ Other: ____

Total Pages Received: ____________________

Documents Submitted to Insurer: ____ / ____

Documents Confirmed Received: ____ / ____

KEY FOLLOW-UP NOTES:

____

____

SECTION 8 – RETURN TO WORK PLANNING

Initial Estimate / Target Return Date: ______________________________

Recent / Upcoming Work Capacity Assessments:

Date Received	Document Type	Provider / Examiner	Submitted to Insurer	Notes	Received?

Notes / Strategy on Returning to Work (Barriers, Adjustments, Supports):

____

____

____

____

____

____

Current / Proposed Return to Work Status Plan:

- ■ Not yet able to return to work
- ■ Reduced hours
- ■ Alternate role
- ■ Pre-injury duties (full capacity)
- ■ Suitable / modified duties
- ■ Workplace adjustments: ____________________
- ■ Employer unable to offer suitable duties (job seeking / retraining)

Actions & Responsibilities (Next Steps):

1. ______________________________
2. ______________________________
3. ______________________________
4. ______________________________

SECTION 9 – CLAIM STRATEGY & MILESTONES

Claim Milestone Tracker

Milestone	Date Initiated	Date Completed	Outcome
Claim Lodged			
Initial Decision			
Liability Accepted / Denied			
IME Scheduled			
Legal Representation Engaged			
Internal Review			
Tribunal / Hearing			
Settlement Discussion			
Final Outcome			

Outstanding Actions Log

Action Required	Responsible Party	Deadline	Completed
		☐ Yes	☐ Yes ☐ No
		☐ Yes	☐ Yes ☐ No
		☐ Yes	☐ Yes ☐ No

Priority Focus:

☐ Urgent Tasks: ____________

☐ Deadlines / Appointments: ____________

☐ Potential Risks: ____________

____

____

____

Risk & Pressure Log

☐ Not yet able to return tto work

☐ Suitable / modified duties:

- ☐ Reduced hours
- ☐ Limited tasks
- ☐ Alternate role

☐ Pre-injury duties (Full capacity)

☐ Employer unable to offer suitable duties (job seeking / retraining).

Actions & Responsibilities (Next Steps):

1. ____________
2. ____________
3. ____________
4. ____________

Personal Position Statement

My Injury Impact Summary:

____

____

My Work Capacity Reality:

____

____

My Current Functional Limitations:

____

____

What Fair Outcome Looks Like:

____

____

SECTION 10 – EVIDENCE & ATTACHMENT INDEX

Evidence Register

Item No.	Description of Evidence	Date Obtained	Submitted to Insurer	Submitted to Lawyer	Confirmed Received	Notes
1			☐ Yes	☐ Yes	☐ Yes ☐ No	
2			☐ Yes	☐ Yes	☐ Yes ☐ No	
3			☐ Yes	☐ Yes	☐ Yes ☐ No	
4			☐ Yes	☐ Yes	☐ Yes ☐ No	
5			☐ Yes	☐ Yes	☐ Yes ☐ No	
6			☐ Yes	☐ Yes	☐ Yes ☐ No	
7			☐ Yes	☐ Yes	☐ Yes ☐ No	

Categories:

☐ Medical Reports ☐ Independent Medical Exams

☐ Imaging (MRI / X-Ray / CT) ☐ Legal Correspondence

☐ Specialist Letters ☐ Email Records ______________

☐ Work Capacity Certificates ☐ Other: ______________

SECTION 11 – TRAVEL & MILEAGE LOG

Travel & Mileage Log

Date	From / To	Purpose	Km/Miles	Parking /	Paid?	Notes
1				☐ Yes	☐ Yes	☐ No
2				☐ Yes	☐ Yes	☐ No
3				☐ Yes	☐ Yes	☐ No
4				☐ Yes	☐ Yes	☐ No
5				☐ Yes	☐ Yes	☐ No
6				☐ Yes	☐ Yes	☐ No
7				☐ Yes	☐ Yes	☐ No

Travel Tips:

☐ Always keep parking receipts.

☐ You can claim tolls too!

☐ You can claim public transport trips.

Attach receipts to this log, photocopy, and keep a copy so you have your records.

Follow-Up Notes:

1. ______________________________
2. ______________________________
3. ______________________________
4. ______________________________

Day __ of 90 Date: ____________ Pain Level (0–10): ________

1. SYMPTOM STATUS

□ Head □ Neck □ Back □ Shoulder □ Arm □ Leg □ Other: ______________________________

Type of Pain:

□ Sharp □ Dull □ Throbbing □ Burning □ Numbness □ Tingling □ Other:

____

Sleep Hours: _____

Sleep Disturbance: Y/N____

Medication / Treatment Used:____

____

2. FUNCTIONAL LIMITATIONS

□ Driving □ Standing □ Sitting □ Lifting □ Household

□ Work duties □ Sleep disruption □ Other: _____

Work Impact Today: ____

Brief Daily Note (1–2 sentences):

____

____

____

____

3. CLAIM COMMUNICATION RECORD

☐ Email to insurer

____

☐ Email from insurer

____

☐ Phone call with insurer

Time: ______ Spoke With: _________________________

____

☐ Lawyer communication

____

☐ No claim communication today

4. SUPPORTING CLAIM ACTIVITY

☐ Rehab / RTW Provider ☐ Medical Certificate Issued ☐ Document Submitted

5. DAILY IMPACT

Impact on daily functioning / mental state:

____

____

____

____

____

____

Day __ of 90 Date: ___________ Pain Level (0–10): ________

1. **SYMPTOM STATUS**

□ Head □ Neck □ Back □ Shoulder □ Arm □ Leg □ Other: ______________________________

Type of Pain:

□ Sharp □ Dull □ Throbbing □ Burning □ Numbness □ Tingling □ Other:

____

Sleep Hours: _____

Sleep Disturbance: Y/N____

Medication / Treatment Used:____

____

2. **FUNCTIONAL LIMITATIONS**

□ Driving □ Standing □ Sitting □ Lifting □ Household

□ Work duties □ Sleep disruption □ Other: _____

Work Impact Today: ____

Brief Daily Note (1–2 sentences):

____

____

____

3. CLAIM COMMUNICATION RECORD

☐ Email to insurer

____

☐ Email from insurer

____

☐ Phone call with insurer

Time: ______ Spoke With: __________________________

____

☐ Lawyer communication

____

☐ No claim communication today

4. SUPPORTING CLAIM ACTIVITY

☐ Rehab / RTW Provider ☐ Medical Certificate Issued ☐ Document Submitted

5. DAILY IMPACT

Impact on daily functioning / mental state:

____

____

____

____

____

____

Day __ of 90 Date: ___________ Pain Level (0–10): ________

1. SYMPTOM STATUS

□ Head □ Neck □ Back □ Shoulder □ Arm □ Leg □ Other: ______________________________

Type of Pain:

□ Sharp □ Dull □ Throbbing □ Burning □ Numbness □ Tingling □ Other:

____

Sleep Hours: _____

Sleep Disturbance: Y/N____

Medication / Treatment Used:______________________________________

____

2. FUNCTIONAL LIMITATIONS

□ Driving □ Standing □ Sitting □ Lifting □ Household

□ Work duties □ Sleep disruption □ Other: _____

Work Impact Today: ____

Brief Daily Note (1–2 sentences):

____

____

____

____

3. CLAIM COMMUNICATION RECORD

☐ Email to insurer

____

☐ Email from insurer

____

☐ Phone call with insurer

Time: _______ Spoke With: _______________________

____

☐ Lawyer communication

____

☐ No claim communication today

4. SUPPORTING CLAIM ACTIVITY

☐ Rehab / RTW Provider ☐ Medical Certificate Issued ☐ Document Submitted

5. DAILY IMPACT

Impact on daily functioning / mental state:

____

____

____

____

____

____

Day ___ of 90 Date: ___________ Pain Level (0–10): ________

1. SYMPTOM STATUS

□ Head □ Neck □ Back □ Shoulder □ Arm □ Leg □ Other: ______________________________

Type of Pain:

□ Sharp □ Dull □ Throbbing □ Burning □ Numbness □ Tingling □ Other: ____________________

Sleep Hours: _____

Sleep Disturbance: Y/N______________________________

Medication / Treatment Used:______________________________

2. FUNCTIONAL LIMITATIONS

□ Driving □ Standing □ Sitting □ Lifting □ Household

□ Work duties □ Sleep disruption □ Other: _____

Work Impact Today: ______________________________

Brief Daily Note (1–2 sentences):

____

____

____

3. CLAIM COMMUNICATION RECORD

☐ Email to insurer ______________________________

☐ Email from insurer ______________________________

☐ Phone call with insurer

Time: ______ Spoke With: ____________________________

____

☐ Lawyer communication ______________________________

☐ No claim communication today

4. SUPPORTING CLAIM ACTIVITY

☐ Rehab / RTW Provider ☐ Medical Certificate Issued ☐ Document Submitted

5. DAILY IMPACT

Impact on daily functioning / mental state:

____

____

____

____

____

____

Day ___ of 90 Date: ____________ Pain Level (0–10): _________

1. **SYMPTOM STATUS**

□ Head □ Neck □ Back □ Shoulder □ Arm □ Leg □ Other: ________________________________

Type of Pain:

□ Sharp □ Dull □ Throbbing □ Burning □ Numbness □ Tingling □ Other:

____

Sleep Hours: _____

Sleep Disturbance: Y/N____

Medication / Treatment Used:____

____

2. **FUNCTIONAL LIMITATIONS**

□ Driving □ Standing □ Sitting □ Lifting □ Household

□ Work duties □ Sleep disruption □ Other: _____

Work Impact Today: ____

Brief Daily Note (1–2 sentences):

____

____

____

3. CLAIM COMMUNICATION RECORD

☐ Email to insurer

____

☐ Email from insurer

____

☐ Phone call with insurer

Time: ______ Spoke With: ___________________________

____

☐ Lawyer communication

____

☐ No claim communication today

4. SUPPORTING CLAIM ACTIVITY

☐ Rehab / RTW Provider ☐ Medical Certificate Issued ☐ Document Submitted

5. DAILY IMPACT

Impact on daily functioning / mental state:

____

____

____

____

____

____

Day ___ of 90 Date: ____________ Pain Level (0–10): ________

1. **SYMPTOM STATUS**

□ Head □ Neck □ Back □ Shoulder □ Arm □ Leg □ Other: ______________________________

Type of Pain:

□ Sharp □ Dull □ Throbbing □ Burning □ Numbness □ Tingling □ Other:

____

Sleep Hours: _____

Sleep Disturbance: Y/N____

Medication / Treatment Used:____

____

2. **FUNCTIONAL LIMITATIONS**

□ Driving □ Standing □ Sitting □ Lifting □ Household

□ Work duties □ Sleep disruption □ Other: _____

Work Impact Today: ____

Brief Daily Note (1–2 sentences):

____

____

____

3. CLAIM COMMUNICATION RECORD

□ Email to insurer

____

□ Email from insurer

____

□ Phone call with insurer

Time: ______ Spoke With: __________________________

____

□ Lawyer communication

____

□ No claim communication today

4. SUPPORTING CLAIM ACTIVITY

□ Rehab / RTW Provider □ Medical Certificate Issued □ Document Submitted

5. DAILY IMPACT

Impact on daily functioning / mental state:

____

____

____

____

____

____

Day ___ of 90 Date: ____________ Pain Level (0–10): ________

1. **SYMPTOM STATUS**

□ Head □ Neck □ Back □ Shoulder □ Arm □ Leg □ Other: ______________________________

Type of Pain:

□ Sharp □ Dull □ Throbbing □ Burning □ Numbness □ Tingling □ Other:

____

Sleep Hours: _____

Sleep Disturbance: Y/N____

Medication / Treatment Used:____

____

2. **FUNCTIONAL LIMITATIONS**

□ Driving □ Standing □ Sitting □ Lifting □ Household

□ Work duties □ Sleep disruption □ Other: _____

Work Impact Today: ____

Brief Daily Note (1–2 sentences):

____

____

____

3. CLAIM COMMUNICATION RECORD

☐ Email to insurer

____

☐ Email from insurer

____

☐ Phone call with insurer

Time: ______ Spoke With: ___________________________

____

☐ Lawyer communication

____

☐ No claim communication today

4. SUPPORTING CLAIM ACTIVITY

☐ Rehab / RTW Provider ☐ Medical Certificate Issued ☐ Document Submitted

5. DAILY IMPACT

Impact on daily functioning / mental state:

____

____

____

____

____

____

Day ___ of 90 Date: ____________ Pain Level (0–10): ________

1. **SYMPTOM STATUS**

□ Head □ Neck □ Back □ Shoulder □ Arm □ Leg □ Other: ______________________

Type of Pain:

□ Sharp □ Dull □ Throbbing □ Burning □ Numbness □ Tingling □ Other:

____

Sleep Hours: _____

Sleep Disturbance: Y/N______________________________________

Medication / Treatment Used:__________________________________

____

2. **FUNCTIONAL LIMITATIONS**

□ Driving □ Standing □ Sitting □ Lifting □ Household

□ Work duties □ Sleep disruption □ Other: ____

Work Impact Today: ____

Brief Daily Note (1–2 sentences):

____

____

____

____

3. CLAIM COMMUNICATION RECORD

□ Email to insurer

____

□ Email from insurer

____

□ Phone call with insurer

Time: ______ Spoke With: ________________________

____

□ Lawyer communication

____

□ No claim communication today

4. SUPPORTING CLAIM ACTIVITY

□ Rehab / RTW Provider □ Medical Certificate Issued □ Document Submitted

5. DAILY IMPACT

Impact on daily functioning / mental state:

____

____

____

____

____

____

Day ___ of 90 Date: ____________ Pain Level (0–10): ________

1. SYMPTOM STATUS

□ Head □ Neck □ Back □ Shoulder □ Arm □ Leg □ Other: ______________________________

Type of Pain:

□ Sharp □ Dull □ Throbbing □ Burning □ Numbness □ Tingling □ Other:

____

Sleep Hours: _____

Sleep Disturbance: Y/N____

Medication / Treatment Used:____

____

2. FUNCTIONAL LIMITATIONS

□ Driving □ Standing □ Sitting □ Lifting □ Household

□ Work duties □ Sleep disruption □ Other: _____

Work Impact Today: ____

Brief Daily Note (1–2 sentences):

____

____

____

____

3. CLAIM COMMUNICATION RECORD

☐ Email to insurer

____

☐ Email from insurer

____

☐ Phone call with insurer

Time: ______ Spoke With: __________________________

____

☐ Lawyer communication

____

☐ No claim communication today

4. SUPPORTING CLAIM ACTIVITY

☐ Rehab / RTW Provider ☐ Medical Certificate Issued ☐ Document Submitted

5. DAILY IMPACT

Impact on daily functioning / mental state:

____

____

____

____

____

____

Day __ of 90 Date: __________ Pain Level (0–10): _______

1. SYMPTOM STATUS

□ Head □ Neck □ Back □ Shoulder □ Arm □ Leg □ Other: ____________________________

Type of Pain:

□ Sharp □ Dull □ Throbbing □ Burning □ Numbness □ Tingling □ Other:

____

Sleep Hours: _____

Sleep Disturbance: Y/N____

Medication / Treatment Used:____

____

2. FUNCTIONAL LIMITATIONS

□ Driving □ Standing □ Sitting □ Lifting □ Household

□ Work duties □ Sleep disruption □ Other: _____

Work Impact Today: ____

Brief Daily Note (1–2 sentences):

____

____

____

____

3. CLAIM COMMUNICATION RECORD

□ Email to insurer

____

□ Email from insurer

____

□ Phone call with insurer

Time: ______ Spoke With: ______________________

____

□ Lawyer communication

____

□ No claim communication today

4. SUPPORTING CLAIM ACTIVITY

□ Rehab / RTW Provider □ Medical Certificate Issued □ Document Submitted

5. DAILY IMPACT

Impact on daily functioning / mental state:

____

____

____

____

____

____

Day __ of 90 Date: ___________ Pain Level (0–10): ________

1. **SYMPTOM STATUS**

□ Head □ Neck □ Back □ Shoulder □ Arm □ Leg □ Other: ______________________________

Type of Pain:

□ Sharp □ Dull □ Throbbing □ Burning □ Numbness □ Tingling □ Other:

____

Sleep Hours: _____

Sleep Disturbance: Y/N____

Medication / Treatment Used:____

____

2. **FUNCTIONAL LIMITATIONS**

□ Driving □ Standing □ Sitting □ Lifting □ Household

□ Work duties □ Sleep disruption □ Other: _____

Work Impact Today: ____

Brief Daily Note (1–2 sentences):

____

____

____

3. CLAIM COMMUNICATION RECORD

☐ Email to insurer

____

☐ Email from insurer

____

☐ Phone call with insurer

Time: ______ Spoke With: _______________________

____

☐ Lawyer communication

____

☐ No claim communication today

4. SUPPORTING CLAIM ACTIVITY

☐ Rehab / RTW Provider ☐ Medical Certificate Issued ☐ Document Submitted

5. DAILY IMPACT

Impact on daily functioning / mental state:

____

____

____

____

____

____

Day __ of 90 Date: ___________ Pain Level (0–10): ________

1. **SYMPTOM STATUS**

□ Head □ Neck □ Back □ Shoulder □ Arm □ Leg □ Other: ____________________________

Type of Pain:

□ Sharp □ Dull □ Throbbing □ Burning □ Numbness □ Tingling □ Other:

____

Sleep Hours: _____

Sleep Disturbance: Y/N____

Medication / Treatment Used:____

____

2. **FUNCTIONAL LIMITATIONS**

□ Driving □ Standing □ Sitting □ Lifting □ Household

□ Work duties □ Sleep disruption □ Other: _____

Work Impact Today: ____

Brief Daily Note (1–2 sentences):

____

____

____

____

3. CLAIM COMMUNICATION RECORD

☐ Email to insurer

____

☐ Email from insurer

____

☐ Phone call with insurer

Time: ______ Spoke With: __________________________

____

☐ Lawyer communication

____

☐ No claim communication today

4. SUPPORTING CLAIM ACTIVITY

☐ Rehab / RTW Provider ☐ Medical Certificate Issued ☐ Document Submitted

5. DAILY IMPACT

Impact on daily functioning / mental state:

____

____

____

____

____

____

Day ___ of 90 Date: ____________ Pain Level (0–10): ________

1. **SYMPTOM STATUS**

□ Head □ Neck □ Back □ Shoulder □ Arm □ Leg □ Other: ______________________________

Type of Pain:

□ Sharp □ Dull □ Throbbing □ Burning □ Numbness □ Tingling □ Other:

____

Sleep Hours: _____

Sleep Disturbance: Y/N____

Medication / Treatment Used:____

____

2. **FUNCTIONAL LIMITATIONS**

□ Driving □ Standing □ Sitting □ Lifting □ Household

□ Work duties □ Sleep disruption □ Other: _____

Work Impact Today: ____

Brief Daily Note (1–2 sentences):

____

____

____

3. CLAIM COMMUNICATION RECORD

☐ Email to insurer

____

☐ Email from insurer

____

☐ Phone call with insurer

Time: ______ Spoke With: ________________________

____

☐ Lawyer communication

____

☐ No claim communication today

4. SUPPORTING CLAIM ACTIVITY

☐ Rehab / RTW Provider ☐ Medical Certificate Issued ☐ Document Submitted

5. DAILY IMPACT

Impact on daily functioning / mental state:

____

____

____

____

____

____

Day __ of 90 Date: ___________ Pain Level (0–10): ________

1. **SYMPTOM STATUS**

□ Head □ Neck □ Back □ Shoulder □ Arm □ Leg □ Other: ______________________________

Type of Pain:

□ Sharp □ Dull □ Throbbing □ Burning □ Numbness □ Tingling □ Other:

____

Sleep Hours: _____

Sleep Disturbance: Y/N____

Medication / Treatment Used:____

____

2. **FUNCTIONAL LIMITATIONS**

□ Driving □ Standing □ Sitting □ Lifting □ Household

□ Work duties □ Sleep disruption □ Other: _____

Work Impact Today: ____

Brief Daily Note (1–2 sentences):

____

____

____

____

3. CLAIM COMMUNICATION RECORD

□ Email to insurer

____

□ Email from insurer

____

□ Phone call with insurer

Time: ______ Spoke With: ______________________

____

□ Lawyer communication

____

□ No claim communication today

4. SUPPORTING CLAIM ACTIVITY

□ Rehab / RTW Provider □ Medical Certificate Issued □ Document Submitted

5. DAILY IMPACT

Impact on daily functioning / mental state:

____

____

____

____

____

____

Day ___ of 90 Date: ___________ Pain Level (0–10): ________

1. **SYMPTOM STATUS**

□ Head □ Neck □ Back □ Shoulder □ Arm □ Leg □ Other: ____________________________

Type of Pain:

□ Sharp □ Dull □ Throbbing □ Burning □ Numbness □ Tingling □ Other:

____

Sleep Hours: _____

Sleep Disturbance: Y/N____

Medication / Treatment Used:____

____

2. **FUNCTIONAL LIMITATIONS**

□ Driving □ Standing □ Sitting □ Lifting □ Household

□ Work duties □ Sleep disruption □ Other: _____

Work Impact Today: ____

Brief Daily Note (1–2 sentences):

____

____

____

3. CLAIM COMMUNICATION RECORD

□ Email to insurer

____

□ Email from insurer

____

□ Phone call with insurer

Time: ______ Spoke With: __________________________

____

□ Lawyer communication

____

□ No claim communication today

4. SUPPORTING CLAIM ACTIVITY

□ Rehab / RTW Provider □ Medical Certificate Issued □ Document Submitted

5. DAILY IMPACT

Impact on daily functioning / mental state:

____

____

____

____

____

____

Day __ of 90 Date: ___________ Pain Level (0–10): ________

1. **SYMPTOM STATUS**

□ Head □ Neck □ Back □ Shoulder □ Arm □ Leg □ Other: ____________________________

Type of Pain:

□ Sharp □ Dull □ Throbbing □ Burning □ Numbness □ Tingling □ Other: ________________________________

Sleep Hours: _____

Sleep Disturbance: Y/N________________________________

Medication / Treatment Used:________________________________

2. **FUNCTIONAL LIMITATIONS**

□ Driving □ Standing □ Sitting □ Lifting □ Household

□ Work duties □ Sleep disruption □ Other: _____

Work Impact Today: ________________________________

Brief Daily Note (1–2 sentences):

____

____

____

____

3. CLAIM COMMUNICATION RECORD

☐ Email to insurer

____

☐ Email from insurer

____

☐ Phone call with insurer

Time: ______ Spoke With: ____________________________

____

☐ Lawyer communication

____

☐ No claim communication today

4. SUPPORTING CLAIM ACTIVITY

☐ Rehab / RTW Provider ☐ Medical Certificate Issued ☐ Document Submitted

5. DAILY IMPACT

Impact on daily functioning / mental state:

____

____

____

____

____

____

Day ___ of 90 Date: ____________ Pain Level (0–10): ________

1. **SYMPTOM STATUS**

□ Head □ Neck □ Back □ Shoulder □ Arm □ Leg □ Other: ______________________________

Type of Pain:

□ Sharp □ Dull □ Throbbing □ Burning □ Numbness □ Tingling □ Other:

____

Sleep Hours: _____

Sleep Disturbance: Y/N____

Medication / Treatment Used:____

____

2. **FUNCTIONAL LIMITATIONS**

□ Driving □ Standing □ Sitting □ Lifting □ Household

□ Work duties □ Sleep disruption □ Other: _____

Work Impact Today: ____

Brief Daily Note (1–2 sentences):

____

____

____

3. CLAIM COMMUNICATION RECORD

☐ Email to insurer

☐ Email from insurer

☐ Phone call with insurer

Time: ______ Spoke With: ____________________________

☐ Lawyer communication

☐ No claim communication today

4. SUPPORTING CLAIM ACTIVITY

☐ Rehab / RTW Provider ☐ Medical Certificate Issued ☐ Document Submitted

5. DAILY IMPACT

Impact on daily functioning / mental state:

____

____

____

____

____

____

Day __ of 90 Date: ___________ Pain Level (0–10): ________

1. **SYMPTOM STATUS**

☐ Head ☐ Neck ☐ Back ☐ Shoulder ☐ Arm ☐ Leg ☐ Other: ______________________________

Type of Pain:

☐ Sharp ☐ Dull ☐ Throbbing ☐ Burning ☐ Numbness ☐ Tingling ☐ Other:

____

Sleep Hours: _____

Sleep Disturbance: Y/N____

Medication / Treatment Used:____

____

2. **FUNCTIONAL LIMITATIONS**

☐ Driving ☐ Standing ☐ Sitting ☐ Lifting ☐ Household

☐ Work duties ☐ Sleep disruption ☐ Other: _____

Work Impact Today: ____

Brief Daily Note (1–2 sentences):

____

____

____

____

3. CLAIM COMMUNICATION RECORD

☐ Email to insurer

____

☐ Email from insurer

____

☐ Phone call with insurer

Time: ______ Spoke With: __________________________

____

☐ Lawyer communication

____

☐ No claim communication today

4. SUPPORTING CLAIM ACTIVITY

☐ Rehab / RTW Provider ☐ Medical Certificate Issued ☐ Document Submitted

5. DAILY IMPACT

Impact on daily functioning / mental state:

____

____

____

____

____

____

Day ___ of 90 Date: ___________ Pain Level (0–10): ________

1. **SYMPTOM STATUS**

□ Head □ Neck □ Back □ Shoulder □ Arm □ Leg □ Other: ______________________________

Type of Pain:

□ Sharp □ Dull □ Throbbing □ Burning □ Numbness □ Tingling □ Other:

____

Sleep Hours: _____

Sleep Disturbance: Y/N____

Medication / Treatment Used:____

____

2. **FUNCTIONAL LIMITATIONS**

□ Driving □ Standing □ Sitting □ Lifting □ Household

□ Work duties □ Sleep disruption □ Other: _____

Work Impact Today: ____

Brief Daily Note (1–2 sentences):

____

____

____

3. CLAIM COMMUNICATION RECORD

☐ Email to insurer

____

☐ Email from insurer

____

☐ Phone call with insurer

Time: ______ Spoke With: ___________________________

____

☐ Lawyer communication

____

☐ No claim communication today

4. SUPPORTING CLAIM ACTIVITY

☐ Rehab / RTW Provider ☐ Medical Certificate Issued ☐ Document Submitted

5. DAILY IMPACT

Impact on daily functioning / mental state:

____

____

____

____

____

____

Day ___ of 90 Date: ___________ Pain Level (0–10): ________

1. **SYMPTOM STATUS**

□ Head □ Neck □ Back □ Shoulder □ Arm □ Leg □ Other: ____________________

Type of Pain:

□ Sharp □ Dull □ Throbbing □ Burning □ Numbness □ Tingling □ Other:

____

Sleep Hours: _____

Sleep Disturbance: Y/N_______________________________________

Medication / Treatment Used:_________________________________

____

2. **FUNCTIONAL LIMITATIONS**

□ Driving □ Standing □ Sitting □ Lifting □ Household

□ Work duties □ Sleep disruption □ Other: ____

Work Impact Today: ____

Brief Daily Note (1–2 sentences):

____

____

____

____

3. CLAIM COMMUNICATION RECORD

☐ Email to insurer

____

☐ Email from insurer

____

☐ Phone call with insurer

Time: ______ Spoke With: ____________________________

____

☐ Lawyer communication

____

☐ No claim communication today

4. SUPPORTING CLAIM ACTIVITY

☐ Rehab / RTW Provider ☐ Medical Certificate Issued ☐ Document Submitted

5. DAILY IMPACT

Impact on daily functioning / mental state:

____

____

____

____

____

____

Day __ of 90 Date: ___________ Pain Level (0–10): ________

1. **SYMPTOM STATUS**

□ Head □ Neck □ Back □ Shoulder □ Arm □ Leg □ Other: ______________________________

Type of Pain:

□ Sharp □ Dull □ Throbbing □ Burning □ Numbness □ Tingling □ Other:

____

Sleep Hours: _____

Sleep Disturbance: Y/N____

Medication / Treatment Used:____

____

2. **FUNCTIONAL LIMITATIONS**

□ Driving □ Standing □ Sitting □ Lifting □ Household

□ Work duties □ Sleep disruption □ Other: _____

Work Impact Today: ____

Brief Daily Note (1–2 sentences):

____

____

____

____

3. CLAIM COMMUNICATION RECORD

☐ Email to insurer

____

☐ Email from insurer

____

☐ Phone call with insurer

Time: ______ Spoke With: ___________________________

____

☐ Lawyer communication

____

☐ No claim communication today

4. SUPPORTING CLAIM ACTIVITY

☐ Rehab / RTW Provider ☐ Medical Certificate Issued ☐ Document Submitted

5. DAILY IMPACT

Impact on daily functioning / mental state:

____

____

____

____

____

____

Day __ of 90 Date: ___________ Pain Level (0–10): ________

1. **SYMPTOM STATUS**

□ Head □ Neck □ Back □ Shoulder □ Arm □ Leg □ Other: ____________________________

Type of Pain:

□ Sharp □ Dull □ Throbbing □ Burning □ Numbness □ Tingling □ Other:

____

Sleep Hours: _____

Sleep Disturbance: Y/N____

Medication / Treatment Used:____

____

2. **FUNCTIONAL LIMITATIONS**

□ Driving □ Standing □ Sitting □ Lifting □ Household

□ Work duties □ Sleep disruption □ Other: _____

Work Impact Today: ____

Brief Daily Note (1–2 sentences):

____

____

____

3. CLAIM COMMUNICATION RECORD

☐ Email to insurer

☐ Email from insurer

☐ Phone call with insurer
Time: ______ Spoke With: ________________________

☐ Lawyer communication

☐ No claim communication today

4. SUPPORTING CLAIM ACTIVITY

☐ Rehab / RTW Provider ☐ Medical Certificate Issued ☐ Document Submitted

5. DAILY IMPACT

Impact on daily functioning / mental state:

____

____

____

____

____

____

Day ___ of 90 Date: ____________ Pain Level (0–10): ________

1. **SYMPTOM STATUS**

□ Head □ Neck □ Back □ Shoulder □ Arm □ Leg □ Other: ______________________________

Type of Pain:

□ Sharp □ Dull □ Throbbing □ Burning □ Numbness □ Tingling □ Other:

____

Sleep Hours: _____

Sleep Disturbance: Y/N____

Medication / Treatment Used:____

____

2. **FUNCTIONAL LIMITATIONS**

□ Driving □ Standing □ Sitting □ Lifting □ Household

□ Work duties □ Sleep disruption □ Other: _____

Work Impact Today: ____

Brief Daily Note (1–2 sentences):

____

____

____

____

3. CLAIM COMMUNICATION RECORD

☐ Email to insurer

____

☐ Email from insurer

____

☐ Phone call with insurer

Time: _______ Spoke With: ___________________________

____

☐ Lawyer communication

____

☐ No claim communication today

4. SUPPORTING CLAIM ACTIVITY

☐ Rehab / RTW Provider ☐ Medical Certificate Issued ☐ Document Submitted

5. DAILY IMPACT

Impact on daily functioning / mental state:

____

____

____

____

____

____

Day __ of 90 Date: __________ Pain Level (0–10): _______

1. **SYMPTOM STATUS**

□ Head □ Neck □ Back □ Shoulder □ Arm □ Leg □ Other: ____________

Type of Pain:

□ Sharp □ Dull □ Throbbing □ Burning □ Numbness □ Tingling □ Other:

____

Sleep Hours: _____

Sleep Disturbance: Y/N____________

Medication / Treatment Used:____________

____

2. **FUNCTIONAL LIMITATIONS**

□ Driving □ Standing □ Sitting □ Lifting □ Household

□ Work duties □ Sleep disruption □ Other: _____

Work Impact Today: ____________

Brief Daily Note (1–2 sentences):

____

____

____

____

3. CLAIM COMMUNICATION RECORD

☐ Email to insurer

☐ Email from insurer

☐ Phone call with insurer
Time: ______ Spoke With: ____________

☐ Lawyer communication

☐ No claim communication today

4. SUPPORTING CLAIM ACTIVITY

☐ Rehab / RTW Provider ☐ Medical Certificate Issued ☐ Document Submitted

5. DAILY IMPACT

Impact on daily functioning / mental state:

____

____

____

____

____

____

Day ___ of 90 Date: ____________ Pain Level (0–10): _________

1. **SYMPTOM STATUS**

☐ Head ☐ Neck ☐ Back ☐ Shoulder ☐ Arm ☐ Leg ☐ Other: ______________________________

Type of Pain:

☐ Sharp ☐ Dull ☐ Throbbing ☐ Burning ☐ Numbness ☐ Tingling ☐ Other:

____

Sleep Hours: _____

Sleep Disturbance: Y/N____

Medication / Treatment Used:____

____

2. **FUNCTIONAL LIMITATIONS**

☐ Driving ☐ Standing ☐ Sitting ☐ Lifting ☐ Household

☐ Work duties ☐ Sleep disruption ☐ Other: _____

Work Impact Today: ____

Brief Daily Note (1–2 sentences):

____

____

____

3. CLAIM COMMUNICATION RECORD

☐ Email to insurer

____

☐ Email from insurer

____

☐ Phone call with insurer

Time: _______ Spoke With: ____________________________

____

☐ Lawyer communication

____

☐ No claim communication today

4. SUPPORTING CLAIM ACTIVITY

☐ Rehab / RTW Provider ☐ Medical Certificate Issued ☐ Document Submitted

5. DAILY IMPACT

Impact on daily functioning / mental state:

____

____

____

____

____

____

Day __ of 90 Date: ___________ Pain Level (0–10): ________

1. **SYMPTOM STATUS**

□ Head □ Neck □ Back □ Shoulder □ Arm □ Leg □ Other: ____________________________

Type of Pain:

□ Sharp □ Dull □ Throbbing □ Burning □ Numbness □ Tingling □ Other:

____

Sleep Hours: _____

Sleep Disturbance: Y/N____

Medication / Treatment Used:____

____

2. **FUNCTIONAL LIMITATIONS**

□ Driving □ Standing □ Sitting □ Lifting □ Household

□ Work duties □ Sleep disruption □ Other: _____

Work Impact Today: ____

Brief Daily Note (1–2 sentences):

____

____

____

____

3. CLAIM COMMUNICATION RECORD

☐ Email to insurer

____

☐ Email from insurer

____

☐ Phone call with insurer

Time: ______ Spoke With: ________________________

____

☐ Lawyer communication

____

☐ No claim communication today

4. SUPPORTING CLAIM ACTIVITY

☐ Rehab / RTW Provider ☐ Medical Certificate Issued ☐ Document Submitted

5. DAILY IMPACT

Impact on daily functioning / mental state:

____

____

____

____

____

____

Day ___ of 90 Date: ___________ Pain Level (0–10): ________

1. **SYMPTOM STATUS**

□ Head □ Neck □ Back □ Shoulder □ Arm □ Leg □ Other: ______________________________

Type of Pain:

□ Sharp □ Dull □ Throbbing □ Burning □ Numbness □ Tingling □ Other:

Sleep Hours: _____

Sleep Disturbance: Y/N______________________________

Medication / Treatment Used:______________________________

2. **FUNCTIONAL LIMITATIONS**

□ Driving □ Standing □ Sitting □ Lifting □ Household

□ Work duties □ Sleep disruption □ Other: _____

Work Impact Today: ______________________________

Brief Daily Note (1–2 sentences):

3. CLAIM COMMUNICATION RECORD

☐ Email to insurer

☐ Email from insurer

☐ Phone call with insurer

Time: ______ Spoke With: ____________________________

☐ Lawyer communication

☐ No claim communication today

4. SUPPORTING CLAIM ACTIVITY

☐ Rehab / RTW Provider ☐ Medical Certificate Issued ☐ Document Submitted

5. DAILY IMPACT

Impact on daily functioning / mental state:

Day __ of 90 Date: ___________ Pain Level (0–10): ________

1. **SYMPTOM STATUS**

□ Head □ Neck □ Back □ Shoulder □ Arm □ Leg □ Other: ______________________________

Type of Pain:

□ Sharp □ Dull □ Throbbing □ Burning □ Numbness □ Tingling □ Other:

____

Sleep Hours: _____

Sleep Disturbance: Y/N____

Medication / Treatment Used:____

____

2. **FUNCTIONAL LIMITATIONS**

□ Driving □ Standing □ Sitting □ Lifting □ Household

□ Work duties □ Sleep disruption □ Other: _____

Work Impact Today: ____

Brief Daily Note (1–2 sentences):

____

____

____

3. CLAIM COMMUNICATION RECORD

□ Email to insurer

____

□ Email from insurer

____

□ Phone call with insurer

Time: ______ Spoke With: _______________________

____

□ Lawyer communication

____

□ No claim communication today

4. SUPPORTING CLAIM ACTIVITY

□ Rehab / RTW Provider □ Medical Certificate Issued □ Document Submitted

5. DAILY IMPACT

Impact on daily functioning / mental state:

____

____

____

____

____

____

Day __ of 90 Date: ___________ Pain Level (0–10): ________

1. **SYMPTOM STATUS**

□ Head □ Neck □ Back □ Shoulder □ Arm □ Leg □ Other: ______________________________

Type of Pain:

□ Sharp □ Dull □ Throbbing □ Burning □ Numbness □ Tingling □ Other:

____

Sleep Hours: _____

Sleep Disturbance: Y/N____

Medication / Treatment Used:____

____

2. **FUNCTIONAL LIMITATIONS**

□ Driving □ Standing □ Sitting □ Lifting □ Household

□ Work duties □ Sleep disruption □ Other: _____

Work Impact Today: ____

Brief Daily Note (1–2 sentences):

____

____

____

3. CLAIM COMMUNICATION RECORD

☐ Email to insurer

____

☐ Email from insurer

____

☐ Phone call with insurer

Time: ______ Spoke With: ___________________________

____

☐ Lawyer communication

____

☐ No claim communication today

4. SUPPORTING CLAIM ACTIVITY

☐ Rehab / RTW Provider ☐ Medical Certificate Issued ☐ Document Submitted

5. DAILY IMPACT

Impact on daily functioning / mental state:

____

____

____

____

____

____

Day ___ of 90 Date: ___________ Pain Level (0–10): ________

1. **SYMPTOM STATUS**

□ Head □ Neck □ Back □ Shoulder □ Arm □ Leg □ Other: ______________________________

Type of Pain:

□ Sharp □ Dull □ Throbbing □ Burning □ Numbness □ Tingling □ Other:

____

Sleep Hours: _____

Sleep Disturbance: Y/N____

Medication / Treatment Used:____

____

2. **FUNCTIONAL LIMITATIONS**

□ Driving □ Standing □ Sitting □ Lifting □ Household

□ Work duties □ Sleep disruption □ Other: _____

Work Impact Today: ____

Brief Daily Note (1–2 sentences):

____

____

____

3. CLAIM COMMUNICATION RECORD

□ Email to insurer

____

□ Email from insurer

____

□ Phone call with insurer

Time: ______ Spoke With: _________________________

____

□ Lawyer communication

____

□ No claim communication today

4. SUPPORTING CLAIM ACTIVITY

□ Rehab / RTW Provider □ Medical Certificate Issued □ Document Submitted

5. DAILY IMPACT

Impact on daily functioning / mental state:

____

____

____

____

____

____

Day __ of 90 Date: ____________ Pain Level (0–10): ________

1. SYMPTOM STATUS

□ Head □ Neck □ Back □ Shoulder □ Arm □ Leg □ Other: ______________________________

Type of Pain:

□ Sharp □ Dull □ Throbbing □ Burning □ Numbness □ Tingling □ Other:

____

Sleep Hours: _____

Sleep Disturbance: Y/N____

Medication / Treatment Used:____

____

2. FUNCTIONAL LIMITATIONS

□ Driving □ Standing □ Sitting □ Lifting □ Household

□ Work duties □ Sleep disruption □ Other: _____

Work Impact Today: ____

Brief Daily Note (1–2 sentences):

____

____

____

3. CLAIM COMMUNICATION RECORD

□ Email to insurer

____

□ Email from insurer

____

□ Phone call with insurer

Time: ______ Spoke With: ________________________

____

□ Lawyer communication

____

□ No claim communication today

4. SUPPORTING CLAIM ACTIVITY

□ Rehab / RTW Provider □ Medical Certificate Issued □ Document Submitted

5. DAILY IMPACT

Impact on daily functioning / mental state:

____

____

____

____

____

____

Day __ of 90 Date: ___________ Pain Level (0–10): ________

1. **SYMPTOM STATUS**

□ Head □ Neck □ Back □ Shoulder □ Arm □ Leg □ Other: ____________________________

Type of Pain:

□ Sharp □ Dull □ Throbbing □ Burning □ Numbness □ Tingling □ Other:

____

Sleep Hours: ____

Sleep Disturbance: Y/N____

Medication / Treatment Used:____

____

2. **FUNCTIONAL LIMITATIONS**

□ Driving □ Standing □ Sitting □ Lifting □ Household

□ Work duties □ Sleep disruption □ Other: _____

Work Impact Today: ____

Brief Daily Note (1–2 sentences):

____

____

____

3. CLAIM COMMUNICATION RECORD

☐ Email to insurer

☐ Email from insurer

☐ Phone call with insurer

Time: ______ Spoke With: ___________________________

☐ Lawyer communication

☐ No claim communication today

4. SUPPORTING CLAIM ACTIVITY

☐ Rehab / RTW Provider ☐ Medical Certificate Issued ☐ Document Submitted

5. DAILY IMPACT

Impact on daily functioning / mental state:

____

____

____

____

____

____

Day ___ of 90 Date: ____________ Pain Level (0–10): ________

1. **SYMPTOM STATUS**

□ Head □ Neck □ Back □ Shoulder □ Arm □ Leg □ Other: ______________________________

Type of Pain:

□ Sharp □ Dull □ Throbbing □ Burning □ Numbness □ Tingling □ Other:

____

Sleep Hours: _____

Sleep Disturbance: Y/N____

Medication / Treatment Used:____

____

2. **FUNCTIONAL LIMITATIONS**

□ Driving □ Standing □ Sitting □ Lifting □ Household

□ Work duties □ Sleep disruption □ Other: _____

Work Impact Today: ____

Brief Daily Note (1–2 sentences):

____

____

____

____

3. CLAIM COMMUNICATION RECORD

☐ Email to insurer

☐ Email from insurer

☐ Phone call with insurer
Time: ______ Spoke With: ____________________________

☐ Lawyer communication

☐ No claim communication today

4. SUPPORTING CLAIM ACTIVITY

☐ Rehab / RTW Provider ☐ Medical Certificate Issued ☐ Document Submitted

5. DAILY IMPACT

Impact on daily functioning / mental state:

____

____

____

____

____

____

Day __ of 90 Date: ___________ Pain Level (0–10): ________

1. SYMPTOM STATUS

□ Head □ Neck □ Back □ Shoulder □ Arm □ Leg □ Other: ____________________________

Type of Pain:

□ Sharp □ Dull □ Throbbing □ Burning □ Numbness □ Tingling □ Other:

____

Sleep Hours: _____

Sleep Disturbance: Y/N____

Medication / Treatment Used:____

____

2. FUNCTIONAL LIMITATIONS

□ Driving □ Standing □ Sitting □ Lifting □ Household

□ Work duties □ Sleep disruption □ Other: _____

Work Impact Today: ____

Brief Daily Note (1–2 sentences):

____

____

____

____

3. CLAIM COMMUNICATION RECORD

☐ Email to insurer

____

☐ Email from insurer

____

☐ Phone call with insurer
Time: ______ Spoke With: ________________________

____

☐ Lawyer communication

____

☐ No claim communication today

4. SUPPORTING CLAIM ACTIVITY

☐ Rehab / RTW Provider ☐ Medical Certificate Issued ☐ Document Submitted

5. DAILY IMPACT

Impact on daily functioning / mental state:

____

____

____

____

____

____

Day ___ of 90 Date: ____________ Pain Level (0–10): _________

1. **SYMPTOM STATUS**

□ Head □ Neck □ Back □ Shoulder □ Arm □ Leg □ Other: ______________________________

Type of Pain:

□ Sharp □ Dull □ Throbbing □ Burning □ Numbness □ Tingling □ Other:

Sleep Hours: _____

Sleep Disturbance: Y/N______________________________

Medication / Treatment Used:______________________________

2. **FUNCTIONAL LIMITATIONS**

□ Driving □ Standing □ Sitting □ Lifting □ Household

□ Work duties □ Sleep disruption □ Other: _____

Work Impact Today: ______________________________

Brief Daily Note (1–2 sentences):

3. CLAIM COMMUNICATION RECORD

☐ Email to insurer

☐ Email from insurer

☐ Phone call with insurer

Time: ______ Spoke With: ____________________________

☐ Lawyer communication

☐ No claim communication today

4. SUPPORTING CLAIM ACTIVITY

☐ Rehab / RTW Provider ☐ Medical Certificate Issued ☐ Document Submitted

5. DAILY IMPACT

Impact on daily functioning / mental state:

Day ___ of 90 Date: ____________ Pain Level (0–10): ________

1. **SYMPTOM STATUS**

□ Head □ Neck □ Back □ Shoulder □ Arm □ Leg □ Other: ________________________________

Type of Pain:

□ Sharp □ Dull □ Throbbing □ Burning □ Numbness □ Tingling □ Other:

____

Sleep Hours: _____

Sleep Disturbance: Y/N____

Medication / Treatment Used:____

____

2. **FUNCTIONAL LIMITATIONS**

□ Driving □ Standing □ Sitting □ Lifting □ Household

□ Work duties □ Sleep disruption □ Other: _____

Work Impact Today: ____

Brief Daily Note (1–2 sentences):

____

____

____

3. CLAIM COMMUNICATION RECORD

☐ Email to insurer

____

☐ Email from insurer

____

☐ Phone call with insurer

Time: ______ Spoke With: ___________________________

____

☐ Lawyer communication

____

☐ No claim communication today

4. SUPPORTING CLAIM ACTIVITY

☐ Rehab / RTW Provider ☐ Medical Certificate Issued ☐ Document Submitted

5. DAILY IMPACT

Impact on daily functioning / mental state:

____

____

____

____

____

____

Day ___ of 90 Date: ____________ Pain Level (0–10): ________

1. SYMPTOM STATUS

□ Head □ Neck □ Back □ Shoulder □ Arm □ Leg □ Other: ______________________________

Type of Pain:

□ Sharp □ Dull □ Throbbing □ Burning □ Numbness □ Tingling □ Other:

____

Sleep Hours: _____

Sleep Disturbance: Y/N____

Medication / Treatment Used:____

____

2. FUNCTIONAL LIMITATIONS

□ Driving □ Standing □ Sitting □ Lifting □ Household

□ Work duties □ Sleep disruption □ Other: _____

Work Impact Today: ____

Brief Daily Note (1–2 sentences):

____

____

____

____

3. CLAIM COMMUNICATION RECORD

□ Email to insurer

____

□ Email from insurer

____

□ Phone call with insurer

Time: ______ Spoke With: __________________________

____

□ Lawyer communication

____

□ No claim communication today

4. SUPPORTING CLAIM ACTIVITY

□ Rehab / RTW Provider □ Medical Certificate Issued □ Document Submitted

5. DAILY IMPACT

Impact on daily functioning / mental state:

____

____

____

____

____

____

Day __ of 90 Date: ___________ Pain Level (0–10): ________

1. **SYMPTOM STATUS**

□ Head □ Neck □ Back □ Shoulder □ Arm □ Leg □ Other: ______________________________

Type of Pain:

□ Sharp □ Dull □ Throbbing □ Burning □ Numbness □ Tingling □ Other:

____

Sleep Hours: _____

Sleep Disturbance: Y/N____

Medication / Treatment Used:____

____

2. **FUNCTIONAL LIMITATIONS**

□ Driving □ Standing □ Sitting □ Lifting □ Household

□ Work duties □ Sleep disruption □ Other: _____

Work Impact Today: ____

Brief Daily Note (1–2 sentences):

____

____

____

____

3. CLAIM COMMUNICATION RECORD

☐ Email to insurer

____

☐ Email from insurer

____

☐ Phone call with insurer

Time: ______ Spoke With: ___________________________

____

☐ Lawyer communication

____

☐ No claim communication today

4. SUPPORTING CLAIM ACTIVITY

☐ Rehab / RTW Provider ☐ Medical Certificate Issued ☐ Document Submitted

5. DAILY IMPACT

Impact on daily functioning / mental state:

____

____

____

____

____

____

Day __ of 90 Date: ___________ Pain Level (0–10): ________

1. **SYMPTOM STATUS**

□ Head □ Neck □ Back □ Shoulder □ Arm □ Leg □ Other: ______________________________

Type of Pain:

□ Sharp □ Dull □ Throbbing □ Burning □ Numbness □ Tingling □ Other:

____

Sleep Hours: _____

Sleep Disturbance: Y/N____

Medication / Treatment Used:______________________________________

____

2. **FUNCTIONAL LIMITATIONS**

□ Driving □ Standing □ Sitting □ Lifting □ Household

□ Work duties □ Sleep disruption □ Other: _____

Work Impact Today: ______________________________________

Brief Daily Note (1–2 sentences):

____

____

____

____

3. CLAIM COMMUNICATION RECORD

☐ Email to insurer

____

☐ Email from insurer

____

☐ Phone call with insurer

Time: ______ Spoke With: ___________________________

____

☐ Lawyer communication

____

☐ No claim communication today

4. SUPPORTING CLAIM ACTIVITY

☐ Rehab / RTW Provider ☐ Medical Certificate Issued ☐ Document Submitted

5. DAILY IMPACT

Impact on daily functioning / mental state:

____

____

____

____

____

____

Day ___ of 90 Date: ___________ Pain Level (0–10): ________

1. **SYMPTOM STATUS**

□ Head □ Neck □ Back □ Shoulder □ Arm □ Leg □ Other: ______________________________

Type of Pain:

□ Sharp □ Dull □ Throbbing □ Burning □ Numbness □ Tingling □ Other:

____

Sleep Hours: _____

Sleep Disturbance: Y/N____

Medication / Treatment Used:____

____

2. **FUNCTIONAL LIMITATIONS**

□ Driving □ Standing □ Sitting □ Lifting □ Household

□ Work duties □ Sleep disruption □ Other: _____

Work Impact Today: ____

Brief Daily Note (1–2 sentences):

____

____

____

3. CLAIM COMMUNICATION RECORD

☐ Email to insurer

____

☐ Email from insurer

____

☐ Phone call with insurer

Time: ______ Spoke With: ___________________________

____

☐ Lawyer communication

____

☐ No claim communication today

4. SUPPORTING CLAIM ACTIVITY

☐ Rehab / RTW Provider ☐ Medical Certificate Issued ☐ Document Submitted

5. DAILY IMPACT

Impact on daily functioning / mental state:

____

____

____

____

____

____

Day ___ of 90 Date: ____________ Pain Level (0–10): ________

1. **SYMPTOM STATUS**

□ Head □ Neck □ Back □ Shoulder □ Arm □ Leg □ Other: ______________________________

Type of Pain:

□ Sharp □ Dull □ Throbbing □ Burning □ Numbness □ Tingling □ Other:

____

Sleep Hours: _____

Sleep Disturbance: Y/N____

Medication / Treatment Used:____

____

2. **FUNCTIONAL LIMITATIONS**

□ Driving □ Standing □ Sitting □ Lifting □ Household

□ Work duties □ Sleep disruption □ Other: _____

Work Impact Today: ____

Brief Daily Note (1–2 sentences):

____

____

____

3. CLAIM COMMUNICATION RECORD

☐ Email to insurer

☐ Email from insurer

☐ Phone call with insurer

Time: ______ Spoke With: ________________________

☐ Lawyer communication

☐ No claim communication today

4. SUPPORTING CLAIM ACTIVITY

☐ Rehab / RTW Provider ☐ Medical Certificate Issued ☐ Document Submitted

5. DAILY IMPACT

Impact on daily functioning / mental state:

____

____

____

____

____

____

Day __ of 90 Date: ___________ Pain Level (0–10): _______

1. **SYMPTOM STATUS**

□ Head □ Neck □ Back □ Shoulder □ Arm □ Leg □ Other: ______________________________

Type of Pain:

□ Sharp □ Dull □ Throbbing □ Burning □ Numbness □ Tingling □ Other:

____

Sleep Hours: _____

Sleep Disturbance: Y/N____

Medication / Treatment Used:____

____

2. **FUNCTIONAL LIMITATIONS**

□ Driving □ Standing □ Sitting □ Lifting □ Household

□ Work duties □ Sleep disruption □ Other: _____

Work Impact Today: ____

Brief Daily Note (1–2 sentences):

____

____

____

____

3. CLAIM COMMUNICATION RECORD

☐ Email to insurer

☐ Email from insurer

☐ Phone call with insurer

Time: ______ Spoke With: ________________________

☐ Lawyer communication

☐ No claim communication today

4. SUPPORTING CLAIM ACTIVITY

☐ Rehab / RTW Provider ☐ Medical Certificate Issued ☐ Document Submitted

5. DAILY IMPACT

Impact on daily functioning / mental state:

____

____

____

____

____

____

Day ___ of 90 Date: ___________ Pain Level (0–10): ________

1. SYMPTOM STATUS

□ Head □ Neck □ Back □ Shoulder □ Arm □ Leg □ Other: ______________________________

Type of Pain:

□ Sharp □ Dull □ Throbbing □ Burning □ Numbness □ Tingling □ Other:

____

Sleep Hours: _____

Sleep Disturbance: Y/N____

Medication / Treatment Used:____

____

2. FUNCTIONAL LIMITATIONS

□ Driving □ Standing □ Sitting □ Lifting □ Household

□ Work duties □ Sleep disruption □ Other: _____

Work Impact Today: ____

Brief Daily Note (1–2 sentences):

____

____

____

____

3. CLAIM COMMUNICATION RECORD

☐ Email to insurer

☐ Email from insurer

☐ Phone call with insurer
Time: _______ Spoke With: ___________________________

☐ Lawyer communication

☐ No claim communication today

4. SUPPORTING CLAIM ACTIVITY

☐ Rehab / RTW Provider ☐ Medical Certificate Issued ☐ Document Submitted

5. DAILY IMPACT

Impact on daily functioning / mental state:

____

____

____

____

____

____

Day __ of 90 Date: ___________ Pain Level (0–10): ________

1. **SYMPTOM STATUS**

□ Head □ Neck □ Back □ Shoulder □ Arm □ Leg □ Other: ____________________________

Type of Pain:

□ Sharp □ Dull □ Throbbing □ Burning □ Numbness □ Tingling □ Other:

____

Sleep Hours: _____

Sleep Disturbance: Y/N____

Medication / Treatment Used:____

____

2. **FUNCTIONAL LIMITATIONS**

□ Driving □ Standing □ Sitting □ Lifting □ Household

□ Work duties □ Sleep disruption □ Other: _____

Work Impact Today: ____

Brief Daily Note (1–2 sentences):

____

____

____

3. CLAIM COMMUNICATION RECORD

□ Email to insurer

□ Email from insurer

□ Phone call with insurer

Time: ______ Spoke With: ___________________________

□ Lawyer communication

□ No claim communication today

4. SUPPORTING CLAIM ACTIVITY

□ Rehab / RTW Provider □ Medical Certificate Issued □ Document Submitted

5. DAILY IMPACT

Impact on daily functioning / mental state:

____

____

____

____

____

____

Day ___ of 90 Date: ____________ Pain Level (0–10): ________

1. **SYMPTOM STATUS**

□ Head □ Neck □ Back □ Shoulder □ Arm □ Leg □ Other: ________________________________

Type of Pain:

□ Sharp □ Dull □ Throbbing □ Burning □ Numbness □ Tingling □ Other:

____

Sleep Hours: _____

Sleep Disturbance: Y/N____

Medication / Treatment Used:____

____

2. **FUNCTIONAL LIMITATIONS**

□ Driving □ Standing □ Sitting □ Lifting □ Household

□ Work duties □ Sleep disruption □ Other: _____

Work Impact Today: ____

Brief Daily Note (1–2 sentences):

____

____

____

____

3. CLAIM COMMUNICATION RECORD

☐ Email to insurer

____

☐ Email from insurer

____

☐ Phone call with insurer

Time: ______ Spoke With: ________________________

____

☐ Lawyer communication

____

☐ No claim communication today

4. SUPPORTING CLAIM ACTIVITY

☐ Rehab / RTW Provider ☐ Medical Certificate Issued ☐ Document Submitted

5. DAILY IMPACT

Impact on daily functioning / mental state:

____

____

____

____

____

____

Day ___ of 90 Date: ____________ Pain Level (0–10): ________

1. **SYMPTOM STATUS**

□ Head □ Neck □ Back □ Shoulder □ Arm □ Leg □ Other: ________________________________

Type of Pain:

□ Sharp □ Dull □ Throbbing □ Burning □ Numbness □ Tingling □ Other:

____

Sleep Hours: _____

Sleep Disturbance: Y/N____

Medication / Treatment Used:____

____

2. **FUNCTIONAL LIMITATIONS**

□ Driving □ Standing □ Sitting □ Lifting □ Household

□ Work duties □ Sleep disruption □ Other: _____

Work Impact Today: ____

Brief Daily Note (1–2 sentences):

____

____

____

3. CLAIM COMMUNICATION RECORD

☐ Email to insurer

☐ Email from insurer

☐ Phone call with insurer
Time: ______ Spoke With: ___________________________

☐ Lawyer communication

☐ No claim communication today

4. SUPPORTING CLAIM ACTIVITY

☐ Rehab / RTW Provider ☐ Medical Certificate Issued ☐ Document Submitted

5. DAILY IMPACT

Impact on daily functioning / mental state:

____

____

____

____

____

____

Day ___ of 90 Date: ___________ Pain Level (0–10): ________

1. **SYMPTOM STATUS**

□ Head □ Neck □ Back □ Shoulder □ Arm □ Leg □ Other: ______________________________

Type of Pain:

□ Sharp □ Dull □ Throbbing □ Burning □ Numbness □ Tingling □ Other:

Sleep Hours: _____

Sleep Disturbance: Y/N______________________________

Medication / Treatment Used:______________________________

2. **FUNCTIONAL LIMITATIONS**

□ Driving □ Standing □ Sitting □ Lifting □ Household

□ Work duties □ Sleep disruption □ Other: _____

Work Impact Today: ______________________________

Brief Daily Note (1–2 sentences):

3. CLAIM COMMUNICATION RECORD

☐ Email to insurer

☐ Email from insurer

☐ Phone call with insurer

Time: ______ Spoke With: ________________________

☐ Lawyer communication

☐ No claim communication today

4. SUPPORTING CLAIM ACTIVITY

☐ Rehab / RTW Provider ☐ Medical Certificate Issued ☐ Document Submitted

5. DAILY IMPACT

Impact on daily functioning / mental state:

Day ___ of 90 Date: ___________ Pain Level (0–10): ________

1. **SYMPTOM STATUS**

□ Head □ Neck □ Back □ Shoulder □ Arm □ Leg □ Other: ____________________

Type of Pain:

□ Sharp □ Dull □ Throbbing □ Burning □ Numbness □ Tingling □ Other:

____

Sleep Hours: _____

Sleep Disturbance: Y/N______________________________

Medication / Treatment Used:________________________

____

2. **FUNCTIONAL LIMITATIONS**

□ Driving □ Standing □ Sitting □ Lifting □ Household

□ Work duties □ Sleep disruption □ Other: _____

Work Impact Today: ______________________________

Brief Daily Note (1–2 sentences):

____

____

____

____

3. CLAIM COMMUNICATION RECORD

☐ Email to insurer

____

☐ Email from insurer

____

☐ Phone call with insurer

Time: ______ Spoke With: ______________________

____

☐ Lawyer communication

____

☐ No claim communication today

4. SUPPORTING CLAIM ACTIVITY

☐ Rehab / RTW Provider ☐ Medical Certificate Issued ☐ Document Submitted

5. DAILY IMPACT

Impact on daily functioning / mental state:

____

____

____

____

____

____

Day __ of 90 Date: ___________ Pain Level (0–10): ________

1. **SYMPTOM STATUS**

□ Head □ Neck □ Back □ Shoulder □ Arm □ Leg □ Other: ______________________________

Type of Pain:

□ Sharp □ Dull □ Throbbing □ Burning □ Numbness □ Tingling □ Other:

____

Sleep Hours: _____

Sleep Disturbance: Y/N____

Medication / Treatment Used:____

____

2. **FUNCTIONAL LIMITATIONS**

□ Driving □ Standing □ Sitting □ Lifting □ Household

□ Work duties □ Sleep disruption □ Other: _____

Work Impact Today: ____

Brief Daily Note (1–2 sentences):

____

____

____

____

3. CLAIM COMMUNICATION RECORD

☐ Email to insurer

____

☐ Email from insurer

____

☐ Phone call with insurer

Time: ______ Spoke With: ___________________________

____

☐ Lawyer communication

____

☐ No claim communication today

4. SUPPORTING CLAIM ACTIVITY

☐ Rehab / RTW Provider ☐ Medical Certificate Issued ☐ Document Submitted

5. DAILY IMPACT

Impact on daily functioning / mental state:

____

____

____

____

____

____

Day __ of 90 Date: ___________ Pain Level (0–10): ________

1. **SYMPTOM STATUS**

□ Head □ Neck □ Back □ Shoulder □ Arm □ Leg □ Other: ______________________________

Type of Pain:

□ Sharp □ Dull □ Throbbing □ Burning □ Numbness □ Tingling □ Other:

____

Sleep Hours: _____

Sleep Disturbance: Y/N____

Medication / Treatment Used:____

____

2. **FUNCTIONAL LIMITATIONS**

□ Driving □ Standing □ Sitting □ Lifting □ Household

□ Work duties □ Sleep disruption □ Other: _____

Work Impact Today: ____

Brief Daily Note (1–2 sentences):

____

____

____

____

3. CLAIM COMMUNICATION RECORD

□ Email to insurer

____

□ Email from insurer

____

□ Phone call with insurer

Time: ______ Spoke With: ___________________________

____

□ Lawyer communication

____

□ No claim communication today

4. SUPPORTING CLAIM ACTIVITY

□ Rehab / RTW Provider □ Medical Certificate Issued □ Document Submitted

5. DAILY IMPACT

Impact on daily functioning / mental state:

____

____

____

____

____

____

Day __ of 90 Date: ___________ Pain Level (0–10): ________

1. **SYMPTOM STATUS**

□ Head □ Neck □ Back □ Shoulder □ Arm □ Leg □ Other: ______________________________

Type of Pain:

□ Sharp □ Dull □ Throbbing □ Burning □ Numbness □ Tingling □ Other:

____

Sleep Hours: _____

Sleep Disturbance: Y/N____

Medication / Treatment Used:____

____

2. **FUNCTIONAL LIMITATIONS**

□ Driving □ Standing □ Sitting □ Lifting □ Household

□ Work duties □ Sleep disruption □ Other: _____

Work Impact Today: ____

Brief Daily Note (1–2 sentences):

____

____

____

____

3. CLAIM COMMUNICATION RECORD

☐ Email to insurer

____

☐ Email from insurer

____

☐ Phone call with insurer

Time: _______ Spoke With: ___________________________

____

☐ Lawyer communication

____

☐ No claim communication today

4. SUPPORTING CLAIM ACTIVITY

☐ Rehab / RTW Provider ☐ Medical Certificate Issued ☐ Document Submitted

5. DAILY IMPACT

Impact on daily functioning / mental state:

____

____

____

____

____

____

Day ___ of 90 Date: ___________ Pain Level (0–10): ________

1. **SYMPTOM STATUS**

□ Head □ Neck □ Back □ Shoulder □ Arm □ Leg □ Other: ______________________________

Type of Pain:

□ Sharp □ Dull □ Throbbing □ Burning □ Numbness □ Tingling □ Other:

____

Sleep Hours: _____

Sleep Disturbance: Y/N____

Medication / Treatment Used:____

2. **FUNCTIONAL LIMITATIONS**

□ Driving □ Standing □ Sitting □ Lifting □ Household

□ Work duties □ Sleep disruption □ Other: _____

Work Impact Today: ____

Brief Daily Note (1–2 sentences):

____

____

____

3. CLAIM COMMUNICATION RECORD

□ Email to insurer

□ Email from insurer

□ Phone call with insurer

Time: _______ Spoke With: ___________________________

□ Lawyer communication

□ No claim communication today

4. SUPPORTING CLAIM ACTIVITY

□ Rehab / RTW Provider □ Medical Certificate Issued □ Document Submitted

5. DAILY IMPACT

Impact on daily functioning / mental state:

____

____

____

____

____

____

Day ___ of 90 Date: ____________ Pain Level (0–10): ________

1. **SYMPTOM STATUS**

□ Head □ Neck □ Back □ Shoulder □ Arm □ Leg □ Other: ______________________________

Type of Pain:

□ Sharp □ Dull □ Throbbing □ Burning □ Numbness □ Tingling □ Other:

____

Sleep Hours: _____

Sleep Disturbance: Y/N____

Medication / Treatment Used:____

____

2. **FUNCTIONAL LIMITATIONS**

□ Driving □ Standing □ Sitting □ Lifting □ Household

□ Work duties □ Sleep disruption □ Other: _____

Work Impact Today: ____

Brief Daily Note (1–2 sentences):

____

____

____

____

3. CLAIM COMMUNICATION RECORD

□ Email to insurer

____

□ Email from insurer

____

□ Phone call with insurer

Time: ______ Spoke With: ______________________________

____

□ Lawyer communication

____

□ No claim communication today

4. SUPPORTING CLAIM ACTIVITY

□ Rehab / RTW Provider □ Medical Certificate Issued □ Document Submitted

5. DAILY IMPACT

Impact on daily functioning / mental state:

____

____

____

____

____

____

Day __ of 90 Date: ___________ Pain Level (0–10): _______

1. **SYMPTOM STATUS**

□ Head □ Neck □ Back □ Shoulder □ Arm □ Leg □ Other: ____________________________

Type of Pain:

□ Sharp □ Dull □ Throbbing □ Burning □ Numbness □ Tingling □ Other:

____

Sleep Hours: _____

Sleep Disturbance: Y/N____

Medication / Treatment Used:____

____

2. **FUNCTIONAL LIMITATIONS**

□ Driving □ Standing □ Sitting □ Lifting □ Household

□ Work duties □ Sleep disruption □ Other: _____

Work Impact Today: ____

Brief Daily Note (1–2 sentences):

____

____

____

____

3. CLAIM COMMUNICATION RECORD

☐ Email to insurer

____

☐ Email from insurer

____

☐ Phone call with insurer

Time: ______ Spoke With: ___________________________

____

☐ Lawyer communication

____

☐ No claim communication today

4. SUPPORTING CLAIM ACTIVITY

☐ Rehab / RTW Provider ☐ Medical Certificate Issued ☐ Document Submitted

5. DAILY IMPACT

Impact on daily functioning / mental state:

____

____

____

____

____

____

Day ___ of 90 Date: ____________ Pain Level (0–10): _________

1. **SYMPTOM STATUS**

□ Head □ Neck □ Back □ Shoulder □ Arm □ Leg □ Other: ________________________________

Type of Pain:

□ Sharp □ Dull □ Throbbing □ Burning □ Numbness □ Tingling □ Other:

____

Sleep Hours: _____

Sleep Disturbance: Y/N____

Medication / Treatment Used:____

____

2. **FUNCTIONAL LIMITATIONS**

□ Driving □ Standing □ Sitting □ Lifting □ Household

□ Work duties □ Sleep disruption □ Other: _____

Work Impact Today: ____

Brief Daily Note (1–2 sentences):

____

____

____

3. CLAIM COMMUNICATION RECORD

☐ Email to insurer

____

☐ Email from insurer

____

☐ Phone call with insurer

Time: _______ Spoke With: ___________________________

____

☐ Lawyer communication

____

☐ No claim communication today

4. SUPPORTING CLAIM ACTIVITY

☐ Rehab / RTW Provider ☐ Medical Certificate Issued ☐ Document Submitted

5. DAILY IMPACT

Impact on daily functioning / mental state:

____

____

____

____

____

____

Day __ of 90 Date: ___________ Pain Level (0–10): ________

1. **SYMPTOM STATUS**

□ Head □ Neck □ Back □ Shoulder □ Arm □ Leg □ Other: ____________________

Type of Pain:

□ Sharp □ Dull □ Throbbing □ Burning □ Numbness □ Tingling □ Other:

____

Sleep Hours: _____

Sleep Disturbance: Y/N______________________________

Medication / Treatment Used:______________________________

____

2. **FUNCTIONAL LIMITATIONS**

□ Driving □ Standing □ Sitting □ Lifting □ Household

□ Work duties □ Sleep disruption □ Other: _____

Work Impact Today: ______________________________

Brief Daily Note (1–2 sentences):

____

____

____

3. CLAIM COMMUNICATION RECORD

☐ Email to insurer

____

☐ Email from insurer

____

☐ Phone call with insurer

Time: ______ Spoke With: ________________________

____

☐ Lawyer communication

____

☐ No claim communication today

4. SUPPORTING CLAIM ACTIVITY

☐ Rehab / RTW Provider ☐ Medical Certificate Issued ☐ Document Submitted

5. DAILY IMPACT

Impact on daily functioning / mental state:

____

____

____

____

____

____

Day ___ of 90 Date: ____________ Pain Level (0–10): ________

1. **SYMPTOM STATUS**

☐ Head ☐ Neck ☐ Back ☐ Shoulder ☐ Arm ☐ Leg ☐ Other: ______________________________

Type of Pain:

☐ Sharp ☐ Dull ☐ Throbbing ☐ Burning ☐ Numbness ☐ Tingling ☐ Other:

____

Sleep Hours: _____

Sleep Disturbance: Y/N____

Medication / Treatment Used:____

____

2. **FUNCTIONAL LIMITATIONS**

☐ Driving ☐ Standing ☐ Sitting ☐ Lifting ☐ Household

☐ Work duties ☐ Sleep disruption ☐ Other: _____

Work Impact Today: ____

Brief Daily Note (1–2 sentences):

____

____

____

____

3. CLAIM COMMUNICATION RECORD

☐ Email to insurer

____

☐ Email from insurer

____

☐ Phone call with insurer

Time: ______ Spoke With: ________________________

____

☐ Lawyer communication

____

☐ No claim communication today

4. SUPPORTING CLAIM ACTIVITY

☐ Rehab / RTW Provider ☐ Medical Certificate Issued ☐ Document Submitted

5. DAILY IMPACT

Impact on daily functioning / mental state:

____

____

____

____

____

____

Day __ of 90 Date: ___________ Pain Level (0–10): ________

1. **SYMPTOM STATUS**

□ Head □ Neck □ Back □ Shoulder □ Arm □ Leg □ Other: ______________________________

Type of Pain:

□ Sharp □ Dull □ Throbbing □ Burning □ Numbness □ Tingling □ Other:

____

Sleep Hours: _____

Sleep Disturbance: Y/N____

Medication / Treatment Used:____

____

2. **FUNCTIONAL LIMITATIONS**

□ Driving □ Standing □ Sitting □ Lifting □ Household

□ Work duties □ Sleep disruption □ Other: _____

Work Impact Today: ____

Brief Daily Note (1–2 sentences):

____

____

____

____

3. CLAIM COMMUNICATION RECORD

☐ Email to insurer

____

☐ Email from insurer

____

☐ Phone call with insurer

Time: ______ Spoke With: __________________________

____

☐ Lawyer communication

____

☐ No claim communication today

4. SUPPORTING CLAIM ACTIVITY

☐ Rehab / RTW Provider ☐ Medical Certificate Issued ☐ Document Submitted

5. DAILY IMPACT

Impact on daily functioning / mental state:

____

____

____

____

____

____

Day ___ of 90 Date: ___________ Pain Level (0–10): ________

1. SYMPTOM STATUS

□ Head □ Neck □ Back □ Shoulder □ Arm □ Leg □ Other: ______________________________

Type of Pain:

□ Sharp □ Dull □ Throbbing □ Burning □ Numbness □ Tingling □ Other:

____

Sleep Hours: _____

Sleep Disturbance: Y/N____

Medication / Treatment Used:____

____

2. FUNCTIONAL LIMITATIONS

□ Driving □ Standing □ Sitting □ Lifting □ Household

□ Work duties □ Sleep disruption □ Other: _____

Work Impact Today: ____

Brief Daily Note (1–2 sentences):

____

____

____

____

3. CLAIM COMMUNICATION RECORD

☐ Email to insurer

☐ Email from insurer

☐ Phone call with insurer

Time: _______ Spoke With: ______________________________

☐ Lawyer communication

☐ No claim communication today

4. SUPPORTING CLAIM ACTIVITY

☐ Rehab / RTW Provider ☐ Medical Certificate Issued ☐ Document Submitted

5. DAILY IMPACT

Impact on daily functioning / mental state:

____

____

____

____

____

____

Day ___ of 90 Date: ___________ Pain Level (0–10): ________

1. **SYMPTOM STATUS**

□ Head □ Neck □ Back □ Shoulder □ Arm □ Leg □ Other: ______________________________

Type of Pain:

□ Sharp □ Dull □ Throbbing □ Burning □ Numbness □ Tingling □ Other:

____

Sleep Hours: _____

Sleep Disturbance: Y/N____

Medication / Treatment Used:_______________________________________

____

2. **FUNCTIONAL LIMITATIONS**

□ Driving □ Standing □ Sitting □ Lifting □ Household

□ Work duties □ Sleep disruption □ Other: _____

Work Impact Today: ____

Brief Daily Note (1–2 sentences):

____

____

____

3. CLAIM COMMUNICATION RECORD

□ Email to insurer

□ Email from insurer

□ Phone call with insurer

Time: ______ Spoke With: __________________________

□ Lawyer communication

□ No claim communication today

4. SUPPORTING CLAIM ACTIVITY

□ Rehab / RTW Provider □ Medical Certificate Issued □ Document Submitted

5. DAILY IMPACT

Impact on daily functioning / mental state:

____

____

____

____

____

____

Day ___ of 90 Date: ____________ Pain Level (0–10): _________

1. **SYMPTOM STATUS**

□ Head □ Neck □ Back □ Shoulder □ Arm □ Leg □ Other: ________________________________

Type of Pain:

□ Sharp □ Dull □ Throbbing □ Burning □ Numbness □ Tingling □ Other:

____

Sleep Hours: _____

Sleep Disturbance: Y/N____

Medication / Treatment Used:____

____

2. **FUNCTIONAL LIMITATIONS**

□ Driving □ Standing □ Sitting □ Lifting □ Household

□ Work duties □ Sleep disruption □ Other: _____

Work Impact Today: ____

Brief Daily Note (1–2 sentences):

____

____

____

____

3. CLAIM COMMUNICATION RECORD

☐ Email to insurer

☐ Email from insurer

☐ Phone call with insurer
Time: _______ Spoke With: ______________________________

☐ Lawyer communication

☐ No claim communication today

4. SUPPORTING CLAIM ACTIVITY

☐ Rehab / RTW Provider ☐ Medical Certificate Issued ☐ Document Submitted

5. DAILY IMPACT

Impact on daily functioning / mental state:

____

____

____

____

____

____

Day __ of 90 Date: ___________ Pain Level (0–10): ________

1. **SYMPTOM STATUS**

□ Head □ Neck □ Back □ Shoulder □ Arm □ Leg □ Other: ______________________________

Type of Pain:

□ Sharp □ Dull □ Throbbing □ Burning □ Numbness □ Tingling □ Other:

____

Sleep Hours: _____

Sleep Disturbance: Y/N____

Medication / Treatment Used:____

____

2. **FUNCTIONAL LIMITATIONS**

□ Driving □ Standing □ Sitting □ Lifting □ Household

□ Work duties □ Sleep disruption □ Other: _____

Work Impact Today: ____

Brief Daily Note (1–2 sentences):

____

____

____

____

3. CLAIM COMMUNICATION RECORD

☐ Email to insurer

____

☐ Email from insurer

____

☐ Phone call with insurer

Time: ______ Spoke With: ___________________________

____

☐ Lawyer communication

____

☐ No claim communication today

4. SUPPORTING CLAIM ACTIVITY

☐ Rehab / RTW Provider ☐ Medical Certificate Issued ☐ Document Submitted

5. DAILY IMPACT

Impact on daily functioning / mental state:

____

____

____

____

____

____

Day ___ of 90 Date: ____________ Pain Level (0–10): ________

1. **SYMPTOM STATUS**

□ Head □ Neck □ Back □ Shoulder □ Arm □ Leg □ Other: ______________________________

Type of Pain:

□ Sharp □ Dull □ Throbbing □ Burning □ Numbness □ Tingling □ Other:

____

Sleep Hours: _____

Sleep Disturbance: Y/N____

Medication / Treatment Used:____

____

2. **FUNCTIONAL LIMITATIONS**

□ Driving □ Standing □ Sitting □ Lifting □ Household

□ Work duties □ Sleep disruption □ Other: _____

Work Impact Today: ____

Brief Daily Note (1–2 sentences):

____

____

____

____

3. CLAIM COMMUNICATION RECORD

☐ Email to insurer

____

☐ Email from insurer

____

☐ Phone call with insurer

Time: _______ Spoke With: ______________________________

____

☐ Lawyer communication

____

☐ No claim communication today

4. SUPPORTING CLAIM ACTIVITY

☐ Rehab / RTW Provider ☐ Medical Certificate Issued ☐ Document Submitted

5. DAILY IMPACT

Impact on daily functioning / mental state:

____

____

____

____

____

____

Day __ of 90 Date: __________ Pain Level (0–10): ________

1. **SYMPTOM STATUS**

□ Head □ Neck □ Back □ Shoulder □ Arm □ Leg □ Other: ____________________

Type of Pain:

□ Sharp □ Dull □ Throbbing □ Burning □ Numbness □ Tingling □ Other:

____

Sleep Hours: _____

Sleep Disturbance: Y/N____________________________________

Medication / Treatment Used:______________________________

2. **FUNCTIONAL LIMITATIONS**

□ Driving □ Standing □ Sitting □ Lifting □ Household

□ Work duties □ Sleep disruption □ Other: _____

Work Impact Today: ______________________________

Brief Daily Note (1–2 sentences):

____

____

____

3. CLAIM COMMUNICATION RECORD

☐ Email to insurer

☐ Email from insurer

☐ Phone call with insurer
Time: ______ Spoke With: ____________________

☐ Lawyer communication

☐ No claim communication today

4. SUPPORTING CLAIM ACTIVITY

☐ Rehab / RTW Provider ☐ Medical Certificate Issued ☐ Document Submitted

5. DAILY IMPACT

Impact on daily functioning / mental state:

____

____

____

____

____

____

Day ___ of 90 Date: ____________ Pain Level (0–10): ________

1. **SYMPTOM STATUS**

□ Head □ Neck □ Back □ Shoulder □ Arm □ Leg □ Other: ______________________________

Type of Pain:

□ Sharp □ Dull □ Throbbing □ Burning □ Numbness □ Tingling □ Other:

____

Sleep Hours: _____

Sleep Disturbance: Y/N____

Medication / Treatment Used:____

____

2. **FUNCTIONAL LIMITATIONS**

□ Driving □ Standing □ Sitting □ Lifting □ Household

□ Work duties □ Sleep disruption □ Other: _____

Work Impact Today: ____

Brief Daily Note (1–2 sentences):

____

____

____

____

3. CLAIM COMMUNICATION RECORD

☐ Email to insurer

____

☐ Email from insurer

____

☐ Phone call with insurer

Time: ______ Spoke With: __________________________

____

☐ Lawyer communication

____

☐ No claim communication today

4. SUPPORTING CLAIM ACTIVITY

☐ Rehab / RTW Provider ☐ Medical Certificate Issued ☐ Document Submitted

5. DAILY IMPACT

Impact on daily functioning / mental state:

____

____

____

____

____

____

Day ___ of 90 Date: ___________ Pain Level (0–10): ________

1. **SYMPTOM STATUS**

□ Head □ Neck □ Back □ Shoulder □ Arm □ Leg □ Other: ______________________________

Type of Pain:

□ Sharp □ Dull □ Throbbing □ Burning □ Numbness □ Tingling □ Other:

____

Sleep Hours: _____

Sleep Disturbance: Y/N____

Medication / Treatment Used:____

____

2. **FUNCTIONAL LIMITATIONS**

□ Driving □ Standing □ Sitting □ Lifting □ Household

□ Work duties □ Sleep disruption □ Other: _____

Work Impact Today: ____

Brief Daily Note (1–2 sentences):

____

____

____

____

3. CLAIM COMMUNICATION RECORD

☐ Email to insurer

____

☐ Email from insurer

____

☐ Phone call with insurer

Time: ______ Spoke With: ________________________

____

☐ Lawyer communication

____

☐ No claim communication today

4. SUPPORTING CLAIM ACTIVITY

☐ Rehab / RTW Provider ☐ Medical Certificate Issued ☐ Document Submitted

5. DAILY IMPACT

Impact on daily functioning / mental state:

____

____

____

____

____

____

Day __ of 90 Date: ___________ Pain Level (0–10): ________

1. **SYMPTOM STATUS**

□ Head □ Neck □ Back □ Shoulder □ Arm □ Leg □ Other: ______________________________

Type of Pain:

□ Sharp □ Dull □ Throbbing □ Burning □ Numbness □ Tingling □ Other:

____

Sleep Hours: _____

Sleep Disturbance: Y/N____

Medication / Treatment Used:____

____

2. **FUNCTIONAL LIMITATIONS**

□ Driving □ Standing □ Sitting □ Lifting □ Household

□ Work duties □ Sleep disruption □ Other: _____

Work Impact Today: ____

Brief Daily Note (1–2 sentences):

____

____

____

3. CLAIM COMMUNICATION RECORD

□ Email to insurer

____

□ Email from insurer

____

□ Phone call with insurer

Time: ______ Spoke With: ___________________________

____

□ Lawyer communication

____

□ No claim communication today

4. SUPPORTING CLAIM ACTIVITY

□ Rehab / RTW Provider □ Medical Certificate Issued □ Document Submitted

5. DAILY IMPACT

Impact on daily functioning / mental state:

____

____

____

____

____

____

Day __ of 90 Date: ___________ Pain Level (0–10): ________

1. **SYMPTOM STATUS**

□ Head □ Neck □ Back □ Shoulder □ Arm □ Leg □ Other: ____________________

Type of Pain:

□ Sharp □ Dull □ Throbbing □ Burning □ Numbness □ Tingling □ Other:

____

Sleep Hours: _____

Sleep Disturbance: Y/N______________________________

Medication / Treatment Used:______________________________

____

2. **FUNCTIONAL LIMITATIONS**

□ Driving □ Standing □ Sitting □ Lifting □ Household

□ Work duties □ Sleep disruption □ Other: _____

Work Impact Today: ______________________________

Brief Daily Note (1–2 sentences):

____

____

____

3. CLAIM COMMUNICATION RECORD

☐ Email to insurer

☐ Email from insurer

☐ Phone call with insurer
Time: ______ Spoke With: ____________________

☐ Lawyer communication

☐ No claim communication today

4. SUPPORTING CLAIM ACTIVITY

☐ Rehab / RTW Provider ☐ Medical Certificate Issued ☐ Document Submitted

5. DAILY IMPACT

Impact on daily functioning / mental state:

____

____

____

____

____

____

Day ___ of 90 Date: ____________ Pain Level (0–10): ________

1. **SYMPTOM STATUS**

□ Head □ Neck □ Back □ Shoulder □ Arm □ Leg □ Other: ______________________________

Type of Pain:

□ Sharp □ Dull □ Throbbing □ Burning □ Numbness □ Tingling □ Other:

____

Sleep Hours: _____

Sleep Disturbance: Y/N____

Medication / Treatment Used:____

____

2. **FUNCTIONAL LIMITATIONS**

□ Driving □ Standing □ Sitting □ Lifting □ Household

□ Work duties □ Sleep disruption □ Other: _____

Work Impact Today: ____

Brief Daily Note (1–2 sentences):

____

____

____

____

3. CLAIM COMMUNICATION RECORD

☐ Email to insurer

____

☐ Email from insurer

____

☐ Phone call with insurer

Time: ______ Spoke With: _________________________

____

☐ Lawyer communication

____

☐ No claim communication today

4. SUPPORTING CLAIM ACTIVITY

☐ Rehab / RTW Provider ☐ Medical Certificate Issued ☐ Document Submitted

5. DAILY IMPACT

Impact on daily functioning / mental state:

____

____

____

____

____

____

Day ___ of 90 Date: ____________ Pain Level (0–10): ________

1. **SYMPTOM STATUS**

□ Head □ Neck □ Back □ Shoulder □ Arm □ Leg □ Other: ______________________________

Type of Pain:

□ Sharp □ Dull □ Throbbing □ Burning □ Numbness □ Tingling □ Other:

____

Sleep Hours: _____

Sleep Disturbance: Y/N____

Medication / Treatment Used:____

____

2. **FUNCTIONAL LIMITATIONS**

□ Driving □ Standing □ Sitting □ Lifting □ Household

□ Work duties □ Sleep disruption □ Other: _____

Work Impact Today: ____

Brief Daily Note (1–2 sentences):

____

____

____

3. CLAIM COMMUNICATION RECORD

☐ Email to insurer

____

☐ Email from insurer

____

☐ Phone call with insurer

Time: ______ Spoke With: ___________________________

____

☐ Lawyer communication

____

☐ No claim communication today

4. SUPPORTING CLAIM ACTIVITY

☐ Rehab / RTW Provider ☐ Medical Certificate Issued ☐ Document Submitted

5. DAILY IMPACT

Impact on daily functioning / mental state:

____

____

____

____

____

____

Day ___ of 90 Date: ___________ Pain Level (0–10): ________

1. **SYMPTOM STATUS**

□ Head □ Neck □ Back □ Shoulder □ Arm □ Leg □ Other: ______________________________

Type of Pain:

□ Sharp □ Dull □ Throbbing □ Burning □ Numbness □ Tingling □ Other:

____

Sleep Hours: _____

Sleep Disturbance: Y/N____

Medication / Treatment Used:____

____

2. **FUNCTIONAL LIMITATIONS**

□ Driving □ Standing □ Sitting □ Lifting □ Household

□ Work duties □ Sleep disruption □ Other: _____

Work Impact Today: ____

Brief Daily Note (1–2 sentences):

____

____

____

____

3. CLAIM COMMUNICATION RECORD

☐ Email to insurer

☐ Email from insurer

☐ Phone call with insurer

Time: ______ Spoke With: __________________________

☐ Lawyer communication

☐ No claim communication today

4. SUPPORTING CLAIM ACTIVITY

☐ Rehab / RTW Provider ☐ Medical Certificate Issued ☐ Document Submitted

5. DAILY IMPACT

Impact on daily functioning / mental state:

____

____

____

____

____

____

Day ___ of 90 Date: __________ Pain Level (0–10): ________

1. **SYMPTOM STATUS**

□ Head □ Neck □ Back □ Shoulder □ Arm □ Leg □ Other: ______________________________

Type of Pain:

□ Sharp □ Dull □ Throbbing □ Burning □ Numbness □ Tingling □ Other:

____

Sleep Hours: _____

Sleep Disturbance: Y/N____

Medication / Treatment Used:____

____

2. **FUNCTIONAL LIMITATIONS**

□ Driving □ Standing □ Sitting □ Lifting □ Household

□ Work duties □ Sleep disruption □ Other: _____

Work Impact Today: ____

Brief Daily Note (1–2 sentences):

____

____

____

____

3. CLAIM COMMUNICATION RECORD

□ Email to insurer

____

□ Email from insurer

____

□ Phone call with insurer

Time: ______ Spoke With: ____________________________

____

□ Lawyer communication

____

□ No claim communication today

4. SUPPORTING CLAIM ACTIVITY

□ Rehab / RTW Provider □ Medical Certificate Issued □ Document Submitted

5. DAILY IMPACT

Impact on daily functioning / mental state:

____

____

____

____

____

____

Day ___ of 90 Date: ____________ Pain Level (0–10): ________

1. **SYMPTOM STATUS**

□ Head □ Neck □ Back □ Shoulder □ Arm □ Leg □ Other: ______________________________

Type of Pain:

□ Sharp □ Dull □ Throbbing □ Burning □ Numbness □ Tingling □ Other:

____

Sleep Hours: _____

Sleep Disturbance: Y/N____

Medication / Treatment Used:____

____

2. **FUNCTIONAL LIMITATIONS**

□ Driving □ Standing □ Sitting □ Lifting □ Household

□ Work duties □ Sleep disruption □ Other: _____

Work Impact Today: ____

Brief Daily Note (1–2 sentences):

____

____

____

____

3. CLAIM COMMUNICATION RECORD

□ Email to insurer

____

□ Email from insurer

____

□ Phone call with insurer

Time: ______ Spoke With: ___________________________

____

□ Lawyer communication

____

□ No claim communication today

4. SUPPORTING CLAIM ACTIVITY

□ Rehab / RTW Provider □ Medical Certificate Issued □ Document Submitted

5. DAILY IMPACT

Impact on daily functioning / mental state:

____

____

____

____

____

____

Day __ of 90 Date: ___________ Pain Level (0–10): ________

1. **SYMPTOM STATUS**

□ Head □ Neck □ Back □ Shoulder □ Arm □ Leg □ Other: ______________________________

Type of Pain:

□ Sharp □ Dull □ Throbbing □ Burning □ Numbness □ Tingling □ Other:

____

Sleep Hours: _____

Sleep Disturbance: Y/N____

Medication / Treatment Used:____

____

2. **FUNCTIONAL LIMITATIONS**

□ Driving □ Standing □ Sitting □ Lifting □ Household

□ Work duties □ Sleep disruption □ Other: _____

Work Impact Today: ____

Brief Daily Note (1–2 sentences):

____

____

____

____

3. CLAIM COMMUNICATION RECORD

☐ Email to insurer

____

☐ Email from insurer

____

☐ Phone call with insurer

Time: ______ Spoke With: ________________________

____

☐ Lawyer communication

____

☐ No claim communication today

4. SUPPORTING CLAIM ACTIVITY

☐ Rehab / RTW Provider ☐ Medical Certificate Issued ☐ Document Submitted

5. DAILY IMPACT

Impact on daily functioning / mental state:

____

____

____

____

____

____

Day ___ of 90 Date: ____________ Pain Level (0–10): ________

1. **SYMPTOM STATUS**

□ Head □ Neck □ Back □ Shoulder □ Arm □ Leg □ Other: ______________________________

Type of Pain:

□ Sharp □ Dull □ Throbbing □ Burning □ Numbness □ Tingling □ Other:

____

Sleep Hours: _____

Sleep Disturbance: Y/N____

Medication / Treatment Used:____

____

2. **FUNCTIONAL LIMITATIONS**

□ Driving □ Standing □ Sitting □ Lifting □ Household

□ Work duties □ Sleep disruption □ Other: _____

Work Impact Today: ____

Brief Daily Note (1–2 sentences):

____

____

____

3. CLAIM COMMUNICATION RECORD

☐ Email to insurer

____

☐ Email from insurer

____

☐ Phone call with insurer

Time: ______ Spoke With: _________________________

____

☐ Lawyer communication

____

☐ No claim communication today

4. SUPPORTING CLAIM ACTIVITY

☐ Rehab / RTW Provider ☐ Medical Certificate Issued ☐ Document Submitted

5. DAILY IMPACT

Impact on daily functioning / mental state:

____

____

____

____

____

____

Day ___ of 90 Date: ____________ Pain Level (0–10): ________

1. **SYMPTOM STATUS**

□ Head □ Neck □ Back □ Shoulder □ Arm □ Leg □ Other: ______________________________

Type of Pain:

□ Sharp □ Dull □ Throbbing □ Burning □ Numbness □ Tingling □ Other:

____

Sleep Hours: _____

Sleep Disturbance: Y/N_______________________________________

Medication / Treatment Used:_________________________________

____

2. **FUNCTIONAL LIMITATIONS**

□ Driving □ Standing □ Sitting □ Lifting □ Household

□ Work duties □ Sleep disruption □ Other: _____

Work Impact Today: ______________________________________

Brief Daily Note (1–2 sentences):

____

____

____

3. CLAIM COMMUNICATION RECORD

□ Email to insurer

□ Email from insurer

□ Phone call with insurer
Time: ______ Spoke With: ___________________________

□ Lawyer communication

□ No claim communication today

4. SUPPORTING CLAIM ACTIVITY

□ Rehab / RTW Provider □ Medical Certificate Issued □ Document Submitted

5. DAILY IMPACT

Impact on daily functioning / mental state:

____

____

____

____

____

____

Day __ of 90 Date: __________ Pain Level (0–10): ________

1. **SYMPTOM STATUS**

□ Head □ Neck □ Back □ Shoulder □ Arm □ Leg □ Other: ______________________

Type of Pain:

□ Sharp □ Dull □ Throbbing □ Burning □ Numbness □ Tingling □ Other:

____

Sleep Hours: _____

Sleep Disturbance: Y/N______________________________________

Medication / Treatment Used:______________________________

____

2. **FUNCTIONAL LIMITATIONS**

□ Driving □ Standing □ Sitting □ Lifting □ Household

□ Work duties □ Sleep disruption □ Other: _____

Work Impact Today: ______________________________________

Brief Daily Note (1–2 sentences):

____

____

____

____

3. CLAIM COMMUNICATION RECORD

□ Email to insurer

____

□ Email from insurer

____

□ Phone call with insurer

Time: _______ Spoke With: ____________________

____

□ Lawyer communication

____

□ No claim communication today

4. SUPPORTING CLAIM ACTIVITY

□ Rehab / RTW Provider □ Medical Certificate Issued □ Document Submitted

5. DAILY IMPACT

Impact on daily functioning / mental state:

____

____

____

____

____

____

Day ___ of 90 Date: ____________ Pain Level (0–10): ________

1. **SYMPTOM STATUS**

□ Head □ Neck □ Back □ Shoulder □ Arm □ Leg □ Other: ________________________________

Type of Pain:

□ Sharp □ Dull □ Throbbing □ Burning □ Numbness □ Tingling □ Other:

____

Sleep Hours: _____

Sleep Disturbance: Y/N____

Medication / Treatment Used:____

____

2. **FUNCTIONAL LIMITATIONS**

□ Driving □ Standing □ Sitting □ Lifting □ Household

□ Work duties □ Sleep disruption □ Other: _____

Work Impact Today: ____

Brief Daily Note (1–2 sentences):

____

____

____

____

3. CLAIM COMMUNICATION RECORD

☐ Email to insurer

____

☐ Email from insurer

____

☐ Phone call with insurer

Time: ______ Spoke With: ___________________________

____

☐ Lawyer communication

____

☐ No claim communication today

4. SUPPORTING CLAIM ACTIVITY

☐ Rehab / RTW Provider ☐ Medical Certificate Issued ☐ Document Submitted

5. DAILY IMPACT

Impact on daily functioning / mental state:

____

____

____

____

____

____

Day ___ of 90 Date: ____________ Pain Level (0–10): ________

1. SYMPTOM STATUS

☐ Head ☐ Neck ☐ Back ☐ Shoulder ☐ Arm ☐ Leg ☐ Other: ______________________________

Type of Pain:

☐ Sharp ☐ Dull ☐ Throbbing ☐ Burning ☐ Numbness ☐ Tingling ☐ Other:

____

Sleep Hours: _____

Sleep Disturbance: Y/N____

Medication / Treatment Used:____

____

2. FUNCTIONAL LIMITATIONS

☐ Driving ☐ Standing ☐ Sitting ☐ Lifting ☐ Household

☐ Work duties ☐ Sleep disruption ☐ Other: _____

Work Impact Today: ____

Brief Daily Note (1–2 sentences):

____

____

____

3. CLAIM COMMUNICATION RECORD

☐ Email to insurer

____

☐ Email from insurer

____

☐ Phone call with insurer

Time: ______ Spoke With: __________________________

____

☐ Lawyer communication

____

☐ No claim communication today

4. SUPPORTING CLAIM ACTIVITY

☐ Rehab / RTW Provider ☐ Medical Certificate Issued ☐ Document Submitted

5. DAILY IMPACT

Impact on daily functioning / mental state:

____

____

____

____

____

____

Day __ of 90 Date: __________ Pain Level (0–10): ________

1. **SYMPTOM STATUS**

□ Head □ Neck □ Back □ Shoulder □ Arm □ Leg □ Other: ____________________________

Type of Pain:

□ Sharp □ Dull □ Throbbing □ Burning □ Numbness □ Tingling □ Other:

____

Sleep Hours: _____

Sleep Disturbance: Y/N____

Medication / Treatment Used:____

____

2. **FUNCTIONAL LIMITATIONS**

□ Driving □ Standing □ Sitting □ Lifting □ Household

□ Work duties □ Sleep disruption □ Other: _____

Work Impact Today: ____

Brief Daily Note (1–2 sentences):

____

____

____

____

3. CLAIM COMMUNICATION RECORD

☐ Email to insurer

____

☐ Email from insurer

____

☐ Phone call with insurer

Time: ______ Spoke With: __________________________

____

☐ Lawyer communication

____

☐ No claim communication today

4. SUPPORTING CLAIM ACTIVITY

☐ Rehab / RTW Provider ☐ Medical Certificate Issued ☐ Document Submitted

5. DAILY IMPACT

Impact on daily functioning / mental state:

____

____

____

____

____

____

Day __ of 90 Date: ___________ Pain Level (0–10): ________

1. **SYMPTOM STATUS**

□ Head □ Neck □ Back □ Shoulder □ Arm □ Leg □ Other: ______________________________

Type of Pain:

□ Sharp □ Dull □ Throbbing □ Burning □ Numbness □ Tingling □ Other:

____

Sleep Hours: _____

Sleep Disturbance: Y/N____

Medication / Treatment Used:____

____

2. **FUNCTIONAL LIMITATIONS**

□ Driving □ Standing □ Sitting □ Lifting □ Household

□ Work duties □ Sleep disruption □ Other: _____

Work Impact Today: ____

Brief Daily Note (1–2 sentences):

____

____

____

____

3. CLAIM COMMUNICATION RECORD

□ Email to insurer

____

□ Email from insurer

____

□ Phone call with insurer

Time: _______ Spoke With: ________________________

____

□ Lawyer communication

____

□ No claim communication today

4. SUPPORTING CLAIM ACTIVITY

□ Rehab / RTW Provider □ Medical Certificate Issued □ Document Submitted

5. DAILY IMPACT

Impact on daily functioning / mental state:

____

____

____

____

____

____

Day __ of 90 Date: ___________ Pain Level (0–10): ________

1. **SYMPTOM STATUS**

□ Head □ Neck □ Back □ Shoulder □ Arm □ Leg □ Other: ______________________________

Type of Pain:

□ Sharp □ Dull □ Throbbing □ Burning □ Numbness □ Tingling □ Other:

____

Sleep Hours: _____

Sleep Disturbance: Y/N____

Medication / Treatment Used:____

____

2. **FUNCTIONAL LIMITATIONS**

□ Driving □ Standing □ Sitting □ Lifting □ Household

□ Work duties □ Sleep disruption □ Other: _____

Work Impact Today: ____

Brief Daily Note (1–2 sentences):

____

____

____

____

3. CLAIM COMMUNICATION RECORD

☐ Email to insurer

____

☐ Email from insurer

____

☐ Phone call with insurer

Time: ______ Spoke With: ________________________

____

☐ Lawyer communication

____

☐ No claim communication today

4. SUPPORTING CLAIM ACTIVITY

☐ Rehab / RTW Provider ☐ Medical Certificate Issued ☐ Document Submitted

5. DAILY IMPACT

Impact on daily functioning / mental state:

____

____

____

____

____

____

Day __ of 90 Date: ___________ Pain Level (0–10): ________

1. SYMPTOM STATUS

□ Head □ Neck □ Back □ Shoulder □ Arm □ Leg □ Other: ______________________________

Type of Pain:

□ Sharp □ Dull □ Throbbing □ Burning □ Numbness □ Tingling □ Other:

Sleep Hours: _____

Sleep Disturbance: Y/N

Medication / Treatment Used:

2. FUNCTIONAL LIMITATIONS

□ Driving □ Standing □ Sitting □ Lifting □ Household

□ Work duties □ Sleep disruption □ Other: _____

Work Impact Today:

Brief Daily Note (1–2 sentences):

3. CLAIM COMMUNICATION RECORD

□ Email to insurer

□ Email from insurer

□ Phone call with insurer

Time: ______ Spoke With: ______________________

□ Lawyer communication

□ No claim communication today

4. SUPPORTING CLAIM ACTIVITY

□ Rehab / RTW Provider □ Medical Certificate Issued □ Document Submitted

5. DAILY IMPACT

Impact on daily functioning / mental state:

Day ___ of 90 Date: ___________ Pain Level (0–10): ________

1. **SYMPTOM STATUS**

□ Head □ Neck □ Back □ Shoulder □ Arm □ Leg □ Other: ______________________________

Type of Pain:

□ Sharp □ Dull □ Throbbing □ Burning □ Numbness □ Tingling □ Other:

____

Sleep Hours: _____

Sleep Disturbance: Y/N____

Medication / Treatment Used:____

____

2. **FUNCTIONAL LIMITATIONS**

□ Driving □ Standing □ Sitting □ Lifting □ Household

□ Work duties □ Sleep disruption □ Other: ____

Work Impact Today: ____

Brief Daily Note (1–2 sentences):

____

____

____

____

3. CLAIM COMMUNICATION RECORD

☐ Email to insurer

____

☐ Email from insurer

____

☐ Phone call with insurer

Time: ______ Spoke With: __________________________

____

☐ Lawyer communication

____

☐ No claim communication today

4. SUPPORTING CLAIM ACTIVITY

☐ Rehab / RTW Provider ☐ Medical Certificate Issued ☐ Document Submitted

5. DAILY IMPACT

Impact on daily functioning / mental state:

____

____

____

____

____

____

Day __ of 90 Date: ___________ Pain Level (0–10): ________

1. SYMPTOM STATUS

□ Head □ Neck □ Back □ Shoulder □ Arm □ Leg □ Other: ____________________________

Type of Pain:

□ Sharp □ Dull □ Throbbing □ Burning □ Numbness □ Tingling □ Other:

____

Sleep Hours: _____

Sleep Disturbance: Y/N____

Medication / Treatment Used:____

____

2. FUNCTIONAL LIMITATIONS

□ Driving □ Standing □ Sitting □ Lifting □ Household

□ Work duties □ Sleep disruption □ Other: _____

Work Impact Today: ____

Brief Daily Note (1–2 sentences):

____

____

____

____

3. CLAIM COMMUNICATION RECORD

☐ Email to insurer

____

☐ Email from insurer

____

☐ Phone call with insurer

Time: ______ Spoke With: __________________________

____

☐ Lawyer communication

____

☐ No claim communication today

4. SUPPORTING CLAIM ACTIVITY

☐ Rehab / RTW Provider ☐ Medical Certificate Issued ☐ Document Submitted

5. DAILY IMPACT

Impact on daily functioning / mental state:

____

____

____

____

____

____

Day ___ of 90 Date: ____________ Pain Level (0–10): ________

1. **SYMPTOM STATUS**

□ Head □ Neck □ Back □ Shoulder □ Arm □ Leg □ Other: ______________________________

Type of Pain:

□ Sharp □ Dull □ Throbbing □ Burning □ Numbness □ Tingling □ Other:

____

Sleep Hours: _____

Sleep Disturbance: Y/N____

Medication / Treatment Used:____

____

2. **FUNCTIONAL LIMITATIONS**

□ Driving □ Standing □ Sitting □ Lifting □ Household

□ Work duties □ Sleep disruption □ Other: _____

Work Impact Today: ____

Brief Daily Note (1–2 sentences):

____

____

____

3. CLAIM COMMUNICATION RECORD

☐ Email to insurer

☐ Email from insurer

☐ Phone call with insurer

Time: ______ Spoke With: ________________________

☐ Lawyer communication

☐ No claim communication today

4. SUPPORTING CLAIM ACTIVITY

☐ Rehab / RTW Provider ☐ Medical Certificate Issued ☐ Document Submitted

5. DAILY IMPACT

Impact on daily functioning / mental state:

____

____

____

____

____

____

Day __ of 90 Date: ____________ Pain Level (0–10): ________

1. **SYMPTOM STATUS**

□ Head □ Neck □ Back □ Shoulder □ Arm □ Leg □ Other: ______________________________

Type of Pain:

□ Sharp □ Dull □ Throbbing □ Burning □ Numbness □ Tingling □ Other:

____

Sleep Hours: _____

Sleep Disturbance: Y/N____

Medication / Treatment Used:____

____

2. **FUNCTIONAL LIMITATIONS**

□ Driving □ Standing □ Sitting □ Lifting □ Household

□ Work duties □ Sleep disruption □ Other: _____

Work Impact Today: ____

Brief Daily Note (1–2 sentences):

____

____

____

____

3. CLAIM COMMUNICATION RECORD

☐ Email to insurer

____

☐ Email from insurer

____

☐ Phone call with insurer

Time: ______ Spoke With: __________________________

____

☐ Lawyer communication

____

☐ No claim communication today

4. SUPPORTING CLAIM ACTIVITY

☐ Rehab / RTW Provider ☐ Medical Certificate Issued ☐ Document Submitted

5. DAILY IMPACT

Impact on daily functioning / mental state:

____

____

____

____

____

____

Day __ of 90 Date: ___________ Pain Level (0–10): ________

1. **SYMPTOM STATUS**

□ Head □ Neck □ Back □ Shoulder □ Arm □ Leg □ Other: ___________________________

Type of Pain:

□ Sharp □ Dull □ Throbbing □ Burning □ Numbness □ Tingling □ Other:

Sleep Hours: _____

Sleep Disturbance: Y/N____

Medication / Treatment Used:____

2. **FUNCTIONAL LIMITATIONS**

□ Driving □ Standing □ Sitting □ Lifting □ Household

□ Work duties □ Sleep disruption □ Other: ____

Work Impact Today: ____

Brief Daily Note (1–2 sentences):

3. CLAIM COMMUNICATION RECORD

☐ Email to insurer

☐ Email from insurer

☐ Phone call with insurer
Time: ______ Spoke With: ___________________________

☐ Lawyer communication

☐ No claim communication today

4. SUPPORTING CLAIM ACTIVITY

☐ Rehab / RTW Provider ☐ Medical Certificate Issued ☐ Document Submitted

5. DAILY IMPACT

Impact on daily functioning / mental state:

Day ___ of 90 Date: ____________ Pain Level (0–10): ________

1. **SYMPTOM STATUS**

□ Head □ Neck □ Back □ Shoulder □ Arm □ Leg □ Other: ______________________________

Type of Pain:

□ Sharp □ Dull □ Throbbing □ Burning □ Numbness □ Tingling □ Other: ______________________________

Sleep Hours: _____

Sleep Disturbance: Y/N______________________________

Medication / Treatment Used:______________________________

2. **FUNCTIONAL LIMITATIONS**

□ Driving □ Standing □ Sitting □ Lifting □ Household

□ Work duties □ Sleep disruption □ Other: _____

Work Impact Today: ______________________________

Brief Daily Note (1–2 sentences):

____

____

____

____

3. CLAIM COMMUNICATION RECORD

□ Email to insurer ______________________________

□ Email from insurer ______________________________

□ Phone call with insurer
Time: ______ Spoke With: ______________________________

□ Lawyer communication ______________________________

□ No claim communication today

4. SUPPORTING CLAIM ACTIVITY

□ Rehab / RTW Provider □ Medical Certificate Issued □ Document Submitted

5. DAILY IMPACT

Impact on daily functioning / mental state:

____

____

____

____

____

____

Made in the USA
Monee, IL
08 November 2026

67816246R00083